The Young Children's Encyclopedia

Volume **16**

Printed in the U.S.A.
Library of Congress Catalog Card Number: 84-82313
International Standard Book Number: 0-85229-426-3

Encyclopædia Britannica, Inc.

Chicago
Auckland   Rome
Geneva   Seoul
London   Sydney
Manila   Tokyo
Paris   Toronto

Table of Contents   Volume 16

VALENTINE'S DAY   Be My Valentine, *pages 6-7*

VALLEY FORGE   The Longest Winter in the War, *pages 8-11*
*A courageous general trains an army and
wins a war for freedom . . . this general
becomes the first president of the United States.*

VAN GOGH, VINCENT   The Man Who Painted Sunflowers,
pages 12-13

VENICE   City of Boats, *pages 14-17*
*Imagine being in a city where the streets are
water and the buses and taxis are boats!*

VERNE, JULES   Journey to Everywhere, *pages 18-21*
*An imaginary journey in a balloon . . . a
pretend voyage to the moon . . . a make-believe
adventure in a submarine . . . these were the
dreams of a famous storyteller that later
came true!*

VIKINGS   The Men of the Longboats, *pages 22-25*

VINCI, LEONARDO DA   The Mystery of Leonardo's Notebooks,
pages 26-29
*Perhaps no other man ever thought about so
many new inventions that later became a part
of the world we live in.*

VOLCANOES   The Soda Pop Volcano, *pages 30-31*

The Smoking Mountain, *pages 32-37*
*Have you ever wondered how mountains grow?
Did you know volcanoes play a part in this?*

VULCAN   God of Fire, *pages 38-39*
*Giant workmen called cyclops . . . a gold
robot and a silver robot . . . all helpers
of powerful Vulcan!*

WASHINGTON, GEORGE   America's First President, *pages 40-41*

WASHINGTON, D.C.   Where Am I?, *pages 42-43*

WATER Waves, *pages 44-45*
Waves can be so strong that they might smash houses, splash as high up as a lighthouse, or toss boats onto the shore!

How Water Gets to the City, *pages 46-49*

WEATHER The Tallest Candle, *pages 50-55*
Loud claps of thunder . . . bright streaks of lightning . . . do thunderstorms frighten you?

Big Winds, *pages 56-61*
Have you ever seen a hurricane or a tornado? Do you know what to do if the weatherman warns that one is coming?

What's a Cloud?, *pages 62-65*

WEAVING Watch the Red Thread, *pages 66-71*

WEEDS What Is a Weed?, *pages 72-73*

WHALES The Biggest Animal of All, *pages 74-79*
Doesn't it seem funny that millions of years ago whales used to live on land and walk around on four legs?

WHEELS Before There Were Wheels, *pages 80-85*

WHERE AM I? Map: Where Am I?, *pages 86-87*
A map to show you different places all over the world that you read about in these books.

WINDMILLS Windmill in Trouble!, *pages 88-91*
A Dutch boy named Piet protects a windmill from a terrible windstorm!

WINGS Wings Everywhere, *pages 92-95*
Wings carry birds and airplanes across the skies . . . wings are used for stopping and starting, for gliding and hovering, for diving and turning.

The Takeoff, *pages 96-99*

WINTER Winter in the Country, *pages 100-105*

WISHES The Magic Sausage, *pages 106-111*

WOLVES How Do You Tell a Storybook Wolf from a Real Wolf?, *pages 112-117*
You remember the story of Little Red Riding Hood . . . well, how do you tell a storybook wolf from a real wolf?

WOOD The Boy Who Couldn't Get Away from Trees, *pages 118-123*

WOODPECKERS Rat-a-tat-tat, What Bird Is That?, *pages 124-125*
It pecks and pecks and pecks all day.

WRECKING Falling Buildings!, *Pages 126-131*

XERXES A Famous King Makes a Mistake, *pages 132-133*
A famous king loses an important battle because he has too many ships!

X RAY A Very Special Picture, *pages 134-135*
An X ray seems magic—it takes a picture through skin or cloth or wood or even metal.

YOU Growing Up, *pages 136-137*

How We Know the World Around Us, *pages 138-141*
Can you name the five senses?

Hiccups, *pages 142-143*

How We Move, *pages 144-147*
Your bones couldn't move if you didn't have muscles—in fact, you couldn't smile or frown without muscles!

Using Your Head, *pages 148-151*
Do you ever wonder how you think—or why you are able to?

ZIPPERS How Do They Work?, *pages 152-153*

ZOOS A Good Place for Animals to Live, *pages 154-159*
Wouldn't it be fun to go to a zoo where the animals don't have to be in cages?

Here are more words
beginning with "V–Z" ... *and* ... Here is where you may
read about them

Venus's-flytrap.................**Plants,** *Book 12, page 112*

Veterinarian....................**Hospitals,** *Book 7, page 150*

Wales..........................**England,** *Book 5, page 94*

Wasp...........................**Insects,** *Book 8, page 32*

Watch..........................**Time,** *Book 15, page 56*

Waves.........................**Water,** *Book 16, page 44*

Wild flower....................**Flowers,** *Book 6, page 80*

Wind..........................**Kites,** *Book 8, page 140*

Water, *Book 16, page 44*

Weather, *Book 16, page 56*

Wizard........................**Friends,** *Book 6, page 140*

Wool..........................**Sheep,** *Book 14, page 58*

Weaving, *Book 16, page 66*

Worm.........................**Earthworms,** *Book 5, page 26*

Weaving, *Book 16, page 66*

Wright Brothers...............**Airplanes,** *Book 1, page 38*

Inventions, *Book 8, page 54*

Zebra.........................**Animals,** *Book 1, page 92*

Zeus..........................**Olympics,** *Book 11, page 128*

Be My Valentine

February 14 is Valentine's Day.
A valentine is a gay card of
    happy wishes.

A valentine is a fancy love
    letter.

A valentine says
    I am thinking of you.

A valentine says
    I love you.

Valentines often have
    paper lace flowers,
    pink roses,
    purple violets,
    shiny green leaves,
    honeybees,
    white doves,
    bluebirds,
    silver ribbons,
    gold wedding rings,
    kittens with big eyes,
    dogs with floppy ears,
    angels with shining faces,
    cupids with bows and arrows,
    and bright red hearts.

Have you ever made your own valentines? Some people think homemade valentines are the best of all.

About all you need is heavy red paper,
plain white paper,
some crayons or paints,
a pair of scissors,
and some paste.

You can cut your paper in the shape of a heart and then decorate it. Or you can color a heart on a square piece of paper. Or you can make it any way you want to. It's *your* valentine—to be sent to someone you care about.

Happy Valentine's Day!

7

VALLEY FORGE

The Longest Winter in the War

Most people have heard the story about George Washington and the cherry tree he chopped down when he was a little boy. But not so many know about the trees he and his soldiers cut down to build log cabins for shelter against the bitter cold of Valley Forge during the American Revolution.

George had grown up to become General Washington. He had been picked by his countrymen to lead their armies in the struggle for freedom from English rule.

In his headquarters at Valley Forge, on a freezing winter night, General Washington picked up his quill pen and wrote by the light of a candle: "We have this day no less than 2,873 men in camp unfit for duty because they are barefooted and otherwise naked. . . ."

These were sad words for a general to have to write about his own army. But they were true words. His soldiers, huddled under thin blankets, were shivering with cold. Some were sick. All were hungry. Many did not have shoes. They had to wrap rags around their feet when they walked in the snow. Some had sticks instead of guns. Some had guns with no bullets.

How could such soldiers win a war and free their country? George Washington must have wondered—especially since many of the American settlers weren't helping him with the war. Many of them did not want to be free from England. Only a few miles away, people lived in warm, snug houses. They had warm clothes and plenty to eat. They trimmed their Christmas trees and sang and danced at parties. And only 20 miles to the southeast the English soldiers, the Redcoats, were snug and warm in Philadelphia. They ate and drank and danced to the sparkle of candlelight and music.

In his sadness General Washington must have thought back to the Christmas night of the year before. That, too, had been a cold and bitter night. The snow had been so thick that the men could hardly see. But that was the night Washington and his ragtag army of farmers and shopkeepers had made their daring and dangerous crossing of the Delaware River to try to catch the enemy by surprise.

Great chunks of ice had floated in the river, banging against the small boats and threatening to sink them. The wind had howled, and the snow had whirled. But silently Washington's soldiers had kept rowing the boats.

On the other bank of the icy river, the Hessians—enemy soldiers paid by the English—had eaten well of Christmas turkey and ham and cheese and rich mince pie. They were not expecting an attack in such cold and stormy weather.

And so they had gone to sleep, not worrying about anything. General Washington and his army had won their first great battle that night.

But now, a year later, the war still had not been won. And on this bitter cold night at Valley Forge, it looked as if it never could be. But Washington did not give up. A Prussian officer helped him train the army, and they drilled night and day. Out of that desperate winter at Valley Forge came an army that was strong enough at last to win the war for freedom. On November 25, in 1783, the last English soldiers sailed away from America.

And on April 30, 1789, General George Washington, the hero of Valley Forge, became the first president of the United States.

You may read about George Washington
on page 40 of this book.

The Man Who Painted Sunflowers

Vincent Van Gogh was a poor Dutch artist who seldom sold a picture. But he didn't care about money—he wanted only to paint life around him as it would look bathed in pure sunlight.

With permission of The Art Institute of Chicago

Finally, he went to the town of Arles, in the south of France. He rented a yellow house that had white walls inside and red-tiled floors. He filled the house with sunflowers, and sometimes he painted pictures of the flowers and other sunlit things in the rooms.

But most of the time he stood outside in the sun and painted the fields and trees, and the people doing their work. Gold seemed to rub off the sun onto his brush and flood his pictures with golden light.

In his paintings, Arles is like no other place in the world. The skies are bluer, and the sun is shinier.

The orchards in bloom are pinker and greener.

The cobblestone roads are more cobbly and stony.

His yellow house is the yellowest house that ever was, and the wild sunflowers he painted are wilder than any you have seen.

Color! Van Gogh wanted color in his pictures. Even his paintings of the night are like the Fourth of July with fireworks spinning all over the sky.

During his life not many people appreciated the paintings of Van Gogh. Now the whole world knows he was a great artist.

There are other stories about artists under Gauguin *and* Goya *in Volume 7 and* Picasso *in Volume 12.*

The National Gallery, London

Courtesy of The Museum of Modern Art, New York City

City of Boats

"Look!" George said. "The streets in Venice are made of water!"

Standing on the stone dock in front of their hotel, the boy and his parents watched the strange boats—*gondolas*—glide past. George and his family had traveled to Venice, Italy, all the way from Canada. They had traveled by plane and train and in a car.

They had found Venice to be different from any place they had ever seen—a city made up of islands connected by arching stone bridges. The streets, called *canals,* were water. The buses were water buses.

The taxis were boats. Long, thin, and high at each end, they floated grandly on the still water as the gondoliers stood tall in their boats, each man moving a long oar.

Now, while one of the gondoliers held his steering pole so his boat wouldn't move, his son, Antonio, helped the Canadian boy and his family get settled in the narrow seats.

Sometimes, when his father was very busy, Antonio was allowed to help steer the long, black boat. Antonio liked to watch the passengers and share their happy excitement. Even though he couldn't understand many of the words, he enjoyed listening to the jumble of happy voices whenever people from other countries rode in a gondola for the first time.

He smiled at George and George smiled back.

"So many, many beautiful buildings!" George's mother said, as they skimmed along the canal.

"It's like a fairyland," George said. "The buildings look like palaces."

"Many of them were built as palaces," his father said. "The outside walls were decorated with small colored tiles."

14

"Some of the palaces are used as museums now," George's mother added. "There are famous paintings and sculptures inside, as well as outside. We can see them later. But right now we're going to a little island where they blow glass."

"Blow glass! What does that mean?" George asked.

"You'll see very soon now," his father answered.

At the island the gondolier's son, Antonio, went with the family to see the glassblowers work. The glass was heated in hot furnaces until it was soft and flowing. The glassblowers blew air into globs of soft glass through a long tube, or *blowpipe,* to make the glass into different shapes. They had to work fast before the glass became cool and hard.

"They've been blowing glass this way for hundreds of years," George's father said. "The Venetians are famous for their glass all over the world."

"Like those colored bottles we saw in the store?" George asked.

"Right. Of course, there are big factories for making most of the glass things we use. But on this island we are seeing how glass things were first made."

As Antonio and George were leaving, a glassblower gave each of the boys a tiny glass horse. They were still warm from the oven.

"Hot from the oven," George's mother said.

"That reminds me, I'm hungry," George said. "May we have lunch in the square? I want to feed the pigeons again."

His father laughed. "Sure we will."

16

The day before, George and his family had sat outside at a tiny table in St. Mark's Square. George had filled his hand with food for the pigeons. When he stood very quietly, without moving, the pigeons flew onto his arms and shoulders to peck the kernels.

When the gondola returned to the dock in front of the hotel, everyone thanked Antonio and his father. The two boys smiled at each other.

"*Ciao,*" George said in Italian.

"Good-bye," answered Antonio.

They waved as the gondola glided down the street of water.

Want to know more?
Read about Canals *in Volume 3,*
Glass *in Volume 7, and* Italy *in Volume 8.*

17

Journey to Everywhere

"Drop a sandbag before you hit the mountain!"
Down goes the sandbag. *Up* goes the balloon.
Imagine exploring a distant land in a giant balloon. You could fly high over mountains and waterfalls, and from your seat in the basket hanging beneath the balloon, you could see the whole land stretched out below you like a giant and colorful bedspread.

You could drift in your balloon over winding rivers, deep blue lakes, and flaming mouths of volcanoes. Or you could peer down on elephants and tigers in jungles.

If it rained, you wouldn't even get wet. You'd just drop some more sandbags, and with the balloon so much lighter you'd rise higher and higher until you floated in the bright sunshine above the clouds.

A man named Jules Verne imagined such a journey many years ago, before anyone had traveled far through the air. He wrote about his imaginary journey in a book called *Five Weeks in a Balloon*.

Maybe you'd rather take a make-believe journey to the moon.

You could stare out of your spaceship's window and watch the Earth grow smaller and smaller, while the moon seemed to grow bigger and bigger.

Jules Verne did just that in his story *From the Earth to the Moon*.

When today's astronauts soar to the moon in their space capsules, they make a journey that Jules Verne imagined long before even the first airplane rose off the ground.

"Look out for the eight-armed octopus!"

"Look out for the man-eating shark!"

"Look out for the giant squid!"

You'd have to "look out" your window, that's all, to see these ocean monsters. At least, you could if you were traveling beneath the sea in an imaginary submarine. In your submarine you could travel all year, deep in the ocean, and spend hour after hour watching a parade of rare and beautiful fishes of different shapes and colors.

Yes, Jules Verne wrote a story about his imaginary adventures —*Twenty-Thousand Leagues Under the Sea*. He named his imaginary submarine the *Nautilus*.

Many years later the first United States nuclear submarine was named the *Nautilus* in honor of the man who had imagined what its journeys would be like.

People have said that Jules Verne invented the future.

He said that he was just very fortunate to live and write in a time when new discoveries and inventions would make such wonderful adventures and dreams possible someday.

Jules Verne believed in his imaginary journeys. Whatever he could *imagine,* he used to say, someone else, someday, would be able to *do.*

If you were going to imagine a journey, what would yours be like?

If you liked this story, you'll like Astronauts *in Volume 1,*
Balloons *in Volume 2, and* Future *in Volume 6.*

The Men of the Longboats

"The Vikings are here!"

When people in the little seacoast towns of northern Europe heard this cry, some were so afraid they couldn't move. Others grabbed up their children and everything they could carry from their houses and ran and hid in the woods. Still others ran down to the sea with spears or rocks or clubs to fight the Vikings.

All this was about a thousand years ago. The Vikings were good sailors and fierce fighters whose homes were beside rough waters in the cold north. They built oar ships to travel from Norway to Iceland and Greenland, where some settled down. Later, daring Vikings sailed farther and farther from home. They built special boats to carry goods to people in faraway lands.

When the Vikings were traders, they were welcomed, for they traded furs and fish and whale oil for whatever things other people had. The ships of other countries did not come to the northland. The Vikings were the only people brave enough to sail far away with only the sun, moon, and stars to guide them. They also knew which foods to eat on a voyage to keep healthy. On board they ate cheese, meat, dark bread, and butter. Whenever they went ashore, they searched for fruit.

The Vikings found that they could be pirates, as well as traders, and steal some of the things they wanted. Their swords were sharp, and in their swift boats they had no fear of pursuit.

For many years the Vikings ruled the seas, sailing along the coasts in boats that looked like sea serpents. They burned towns, stole what they wanted, and even took some people for slaves.

Many of the Vikings were fair-haired and many were tall. In battle they often wore tunics (long shirts) made of iron rings strung together. Their oval shields were made of wood with a metal knob in the center. In their high, pointed helmets, they may have seemed like giants to frightened villagers under attack.

When the fighting was over, the Vikings sailed home, carrying their stolen goods and their captives.

What do you suppose happened to the captured people who became the Vikings' slaves?

New slaves must have been surprised to find that Vikings were not so fierce at home. There, many of them lived quietly as farmers. Viking children could swim and ride horseback and sail boats. There weren't any schools—but when Vikings learned how to write from people in other countries, they made their children learn, too.

Slaves had to serve their masters but were generally treated with kindness. No slave ever was chained to an oar of a Viking ship.

Then the Vikings began taking land from people in other countries. In their new lands, the Vikings tried to live as they had at home. But many of the ways of the new lands became their ways, and in time the Vikings became part of the new countries. They were no longer Vikings!

Yet their stories lived. The stories tell us that Leif the Lucky, the son of Eric the Red, sailed all the way across the Atlantic Ocean before Columbus did. He spent a winter in Vinland, which we know as Newfoundland.

Look at the map on the next page. Everything colored red is Viking land. Did anyone in your family, even far, far back, come from any of these countries?

Then perhaps *you* are related to the Vikings.

Alinari

VINCI, LEONARDO DA

The Mystery of
Leonardo's Notebooks

Five hundred years ago, when the city of Florence in Italy was the home of the greatest artists in the world, a young boy went there to study art.

He was handsome and strong and clever at everything he did. Not only could he paint and draw and make statues, but he could also sing and play musical instruments. And he was a wonderful mechanic. Soon everyone was talking about this boy, Leonardo da Vinci.

"He will grow up to be the greatest painter in Florence," people said. They looked forward to seeing the beautiful pictures he would make.

When he became a young man, people heard that he was starting a painting for the altar of a church. They waited eagerly for him to finish.

But the painting went very, very slowly.

It went slowly because if Leonardo wanted to draw a man or a horse, a plant or a rock or a cloud, he had to know everything there was to know about it. He had to know what the man's muscles were like under his skin and what his bones were like under his muscles.

He made hundreds of drawings in his notebooks. He went to mountains and to swamps and drew the plants and the rocks. He went to the seashore and drew the ocean. He looked at the sky and drew the sun and the stars.

People began to shake their heads sadly.

"He can do everything, but he will never do *anything*," they said. "He never gets started. He is always making notes in his notebooks."

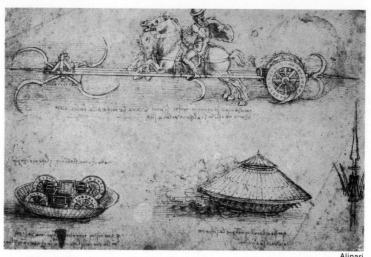

When Leonardo died as an old man, he left two paintings that are famous to this day—the *Mona Lisa* and the *Last Supper*. But he left few paintings, and most of them were not even finished.

He *did* leave a great many notebooks, but they were written in a language that seemed impossible to read. The books had some pretty drawings in them of birds and plants and faces and arms and legs, but they were also filled with strange drawings no one could understand.

Some people thought he hadn't amounted to much.

But finally it was understood that Leonardo's notes were simply written backward and could be read with a mirror.

Then everyone was amazed at what they read!

Leonardo had not been wasting his time making endless notes.

The drawings of birds were not just pretty drawings. They showed how birds could fly—how their wings moved, how they used their tails to guide them, and how they cut down their speed to land smoothly and safely. And the strange drawings were of future inventions that Leonardo had thought of—drawings of an airplane, a helicopter, and a parachute. They were all ideas he had gotten from watching the birds. Many other things we have today

—air conditioning, automobiles, diving snorkels, spinning wheels, machine guns, and tanks—were thought of by Leonardo 500 years ago.

Before anyone else knew how rocks were formed or how the blood circulated in the body, Leonardo knew.

Perhaps no one man ever thought of so many new things that later became part of the world we live in.

*If you liked this story,
you'll like* Jules Verne
on page 18 of this book.

The Soda Pop Volcano

Let's talk about soda pop.
Soda pop is water,
   flavoring,
      sweetening,
         and gas—all mixed up together.
In a bottle the glass presses against the soda pop from all sides
and keeps it quiet.
   When you take the cap off, some of the gas escapes with a
z-z-zip and pushes some of the soda pop out with it in spatters
and bubbles.

Now let's talk about volcanoes.

In a volcano, melted rock and gas are all mixed up together. (Most of it is not the same kind of gas that's in soda pop, but still it's gas.)

Deep in the earth the hard rock presses against the melted rock and gas from all sides and keeps it quiet.

But if the melted rock and gas comes near the top of the ground, some of the gas sometimes escapes with a *z-z-zip* through a hole and pushes some of the melted rock out with it.

So you could say that a volcano is a little like a bottle of soda pop . . . or that a bottle of soda pop is a little like a volcano.

To understand what a gas is,
read Liquids, Solids, and Gases *in Volume 9.*

The Smoking Mountain

A few years ago men on a ship in the ocean saw the water bubbling and boiling. They went closer. Night came before they had seen very much. But in the morning they saw an island where there had been no island before.

It was a very hot island, with smoke, steam, and fire.

Actually, the island was the top of a mountain that had been growing up from the floor of the ocean and had poked through the water into the air.

How does a mountain grow?

If the mountain is a volcano, it is easy to see how it grows. A volcano starts from a hole in the ground from which hot rock and smoke and steam come out. Far, far under the ground it is so hot that rock melts. This hot melted rock, or *lava,* is sometimes pushed out of the earth through a hole or a crack in the ground. The steam inside the earth pushes the rock out.

As more and more rock comes out, it makes a pile that becomes a mountain. Sometimes the rock flows out like hot mush. Sometimes it is shot out in big chunks of hard rock. The more stuff that comes out, the higher the mountain grows.

If the mountain is growing under the ocean, it becomes an island when it reaches the top of the water. The little island that the men saw from the ship started this way. So did the big Hawaiian Islands and the enormous island of Iceland.

Not many years ago in Mexico, a little boy and his father discovered a volcano growing in a cornfield. Smoke puffed up, and rock started popping up out of a crack that opened in the ground.

The boy thought the cornfield was throwing rocks at him! He picked one up. It was hot. He dropped it and ran away frightened. Smoke and rock continued to come from the crack in the ground.

A new volcano was being born.

The volcano in the cornfield grew until it was bigger than the cornfield! Black smoke puffed out. Hot ashes fell like black snowflakes. Hot rock and fire and lava shot out. People called the volcano the Little Monster because it grew so fast. Scientists came from all over the world to study it and watch it grow. It is not often that people get a chance to watch a volcano from the very beginning.

Most of the volcanoes have been here for a very long time. Some have been here so long that now they are cold. They are called dead volcanoes. They have stopped throwing out fire and melted rock and smoke. It is safe to walk on them. Farms are plowed on the quiet slopes, and people have built houses there.

Some volcanoes have stopped throwing out hot rock, but they still smoke a little now and then. They are "sleeping" volcanoes. Sometime they may "wake up."

A volcano named Vesuvius slept for a thousand years. But it woke up and threw out so much hot melted rock that it buried the buildings of two cities.

Today volcanoes are not so dangerous for people as they were a long time ago. Now we know more about *why* volcanoes do what they do, and we can usually tell *when* they are going to do it. Before a sleeping volcano wakes up, it usually makes a noise like faraway thunder, and the ground shakes in small earthquakes. People are warned and have time to get away safely.

People used to think dragons under the earth caused volcanoes. They said the smoke that puffed above the ground was the dragon's breath. They said the earthquakes were caused by the dragon's moving around down in the earth. Now we know that this is not true.

Another thing we know about volcanoes is that they don't happen just anywhere. There are certain places under the earth

where the rock is broken in a way that lets the steam and hot rock escape to the outside more easily. Scientists know where these places are, and maps have been made to let everybody know.

There are different kinds of volcanoes. Some explode so violently that the rock goes high into the air and falls miles away. A volcano may shoot out ashes so high that they float all the way around the world. They have made the sunsets green and the snow purple.

Other volcanoes are more gentle. The hot lava rises in their cones and overflows, rolling slowly down the mountainside, where it becomes cool and hard.

One very tall volcano stays fiery red at the top all the time. It is lucky that the volcano is near the ocean. Sailors can use it for a lighthouse.

Want to know more?
Read "Inside the Earth" *under* Earth *in Volume 5*
and read "How Did the Mountains Get There?" *under* Mountains *in Volume 10.*

God of Fire

Vulcan—great god of fire!

Deep inside smoking volcanoes Vulcan's giant workmen hammered so hard that their pounding could be heard over mountains and across oceans. The sparks from their fires flew as high as the stars. These giants were called *cyclops* and each had only one eye.

Vulcan made gleaming golden thrones for the ancient gods. With skillful hands he shaped glittering jewels to ornament weapons and war chariots.

Although his body was big and strong, Vulcan's legs were weak from an accident. He built two robots—one of gold, the other of silver. These mechanical men carried him to and from his workshops. The robots had mechanical brains and could think for themselves. Vulcan even gave them silver tongues for talking.

Other stories about the gods can be found under Mercury *in Volume 10,* Neptune *in Volume 11, and* Pandora *and* Persephone *in Volume 12.*

America's First President

It was a small, new country ruled by a king who lived far across the ocean. Not many of the country's people had ever gone to school. Few could even read or write. Most families lived in small, crowded houses in settlements called *colonies*.

The world did not yet know how to use electricity, and telephones were far in the future. Messages usually were delivered by riders on horses. The narrow dirt roads ran through woods and were often muddy and deeply rutted. It took a long time to get from place to place. Today we fly around the world in less time than it then took to travel between most towns.

The people worked hard, growing crops for food and cutting through thick forests to build roads and towns. They fought in a war to help their king . . . and in another war to win their freedom from him.

The country was to become the United States. Most of its people had come from England and their king was George III.

There were many men who helped lead this country to freedom —and one of the strongest leaders was George Washington.

Washington grew up on a large farm, where corn, tobacco, vegetables, and other crops were grown. But he loved adventure, and as a young man he roamed far—exploring the wilderness and making maps for other people to follow.

Washington helped the English fight the French for control of this vast wilderness . . . but when the people of the colonies chose to fight England to gain their freedom, Washington sided with them. They then chose this strong, wise man to be their leader— the general in charge of all the colonial armies.

The colonial soldiers won and lost many battles. Often there was no food or clothing. It was cold and lonely. But Washington shared his men's hardships. When the war ended and the people were freed from the king's rule, George Washington was chosen to be the first president of the United States of America.

You may read about another famous U.S. president under Abraham Lincoln *in Volume 9.*

41

Where Am I?

I live in a very important city. It isn't the biggest city in the world, or even the biggest city in the United States. But it's always in the news. And people keep coming here from everywhere in the world.

People make important things here. But these things are not made in factories with tall chimneys pouring out smoke.

What do people make in my city?

They make *speeches*. They make *laws*. And they make *money*.

Let's start with money. People in one big building do nothing but make money. They make millions and millions of dollars of paper money. You can come and watch them print and count the money. Some of it someday may go into your very own pocket.

From all over the United States people come to my city to make laws. These lawmakers, called *senators* and *representatives,* make laws, or rules, for everybody in the country. They meet in a big building with a dome, and sometimes they make speeches. The building is called the Capitol.

In front of the Capitol is a very wide street, and other beautiful streets go out from the Capitol building like spokes in a wheel. In the spring the river's edge and many of the streets are pink and glowing with the blossoms of cherry trees, a gift from the people of Japan.

One of the famous buildings near the Capitol is called the White House. The president of the United States and his family live there.

A tall monument pointing to the sky was built to honor the first president—George Washington. You can ride in an elevator to the top of the Washington Monument. From this high place you can look all around the city. You will see monuments that honor other presidents—Jefferson and Lincoln.

By now you surely know where I live—Washington, D.C.

Look under Where Am I? *in Volume 16 and find Washington, D.C., on the map.*

Waves

The ocean is never still. It is always moving. What do you suppose makes it move?

Not the fish that swim in the ocean, although there are billions of them, and some are very big.

Not the ships that sail the ocean, although they are bigger than the fish.

The thing that makes the ocean move and change so that it looks different almost every second is the wind. A gentle wind makes soft, slow waves that float bubbles around your feet and knees.

Stronger winds make waves that go over your head.

Big, storm winds make waves so big and strong that they can smash oceanside houses into splinters of wood.

44

Storm winds can make waves that splash to the top of a lighthouse.

They can make waves that toss boats up onto the shore.

A wave is water moving up and down. No matter how high the water piles up, it has to come down.

The last wave—the one next to the shore—doesn't pile up again as the other waves do. The land won't let it. The land breaks it. We call these last waves *breakers*. They sort of fall over on their faces and make a big splash.

Breakers are fun to play in. They give us our "free rides" to shore. But when the lifeguard tells us the breakers are too big and strong, it's time to pack up and go home. It's time to say to the ocean, "We'll see you again when you're not playing so rough."

Want to know more?
Read about the Ocean *in Volume 11.*

How Water Gets to the City

This deer lives in a forest of whispering trees.

This boy lives near the center of a great, booming city.

Both the boy and the deer are drinking water from the same shining mountain lake!

How can they both do this?

The deer simply follows the path that hundreds of deer have made through the forest to the lake—and drinks.

When the boy is thirsty he turns on the faucet over the kitchen sink and fills his glass. That seems simple, too. But making water run from a faraway mountain lake to the center of a city is a big job for even the best engineers.

Sometime you may see from a distance a pretty little river. But if you look at it up close, you'll see that it is a very different kind of river. It is paved on the bottom and sides with neatly fitted bricks. It is a river made by men. It leads the water from a mountain lake to New York City. Such a man-made river is called an *aqueduct.*

If you were to follow this river, you would find a certain place where the water tumbles into a big tunnel. Under the ground the tunnel turns and twists like the longest snake you could imagine. The water flows through the turning, twisting tunnel and finally goes into some pipes. Now the water is getting near the city. Soon it may pour out of a faucet or shower nozzle in someone's kitchen or bathroom, or through a fire hydrant into a hose spraying a blazing fire.

Long ago when there were not very many people on the Earth, most people made their homes close to rivers or ponds or streams. They drank and washed and bathed and cooked with this water. When it was all used up— or got too dirty—these long-ago people just packed up and moved to another place near water.

People finally learned to build houses that had strong walls and a floor and a roof. They invented many, many things to go into their houses—furniture, stoves, refrigerators. They built factories to make all these things. At the same time, they built schools and office buildings and, always, more houses.

Now our way of living is much easier and more comfortable than that of people who lived thousands of years ago.

But now we cannot move our homes to water. We must move the water to our homes.

And we do!

Because water from mountain lakes is usually the purest and cleanest and best tasting, many cities get their water from such lakes. Uphill and downhill, the water may flow for hundreds of miles through giant pipes, from the lake to the city.

Other cities pump water from deep under the ground. But many cities must take water from a dirty river or lake. This water must be cleaned before it can be used. These cities build filtration plants. The filtration plants look like factories and are as busy as factories. They are filled with machines that strain dirt and germs from the water.

It is hard work to give clean water to a city. But we have to do it. Without water we could not have a city.

Next time you take a shower, think back through the journey the water may have taken—through pipes and tunnels, aqueducts, a filtration plant—think back, back, back to some river or lake or reservoir miles and miles away from your handy faucets marked *Hot* and *Cold*.

If you would like to learn about
the underwater passages the water goes through,
look up Tunnels *in Volume 15.*

The Tallest Candle

Crash!

The thunder banged and rumbled over the playground. The children ran for the shelter house—all except Carol, who ran toward a tall shade tree. Her father had put a white cardboard box on a picnic table under the tree. Inside the box was a big birthday cake with pink frosting and "Happy Birthday, Carol" written on it.

Before she reached the tree, Carol's father shouted, "Carol! Come to the shelter house!"

Then it really began to pour, and the lightning flashed and the thunder rumbled. Carol forgot all about the birthday box. She turned and ran the other way.

Her father ran to meet her. He took her little hand in his big one, and together they ran through the rain the rest of the way to the shelter house.

As soon as she could catch her breath, Carol asked her mother, "Did you get the cake? Did you?"

Carol's mother and father looked at each other. In the excitement they had forgotten the cake.

"It's too late now," said her father.

Just then there was a loud *crash!*

"The tree!" shouted one of the boys. "It sounded as if it hit the tree by the picnic table!"

50

"What sounded as if it hit the tree?" Carol's father asked.

"The thunder," said the boy.

Carol's father went to the window. "The tree wasn't hit," he said. "And anyway, *thunder* doesn't hit trees."

"Then what does hit trees?" Carol asked.

"Lightning sometimes hits trees," her father answered. "Thunder is the noise you hear when a bolt of lightning leaves a cloud. Thunder can never hurt you. And by the time you hear the thunder, the lightning is already gone."

There was another flash and an even louder *crash*, followed by the rumbliest rumble of all.

"That was very close," Carol's father said.

One of the girls near the window cried, "Look! That time the lightning *did* hit the tree!"

All of the children crowded around the window to see the tree. One of the top branches not far from the picnic table was split and burning. The rain soon put the fire out, and the black end of the branch smoked for a few minutes.

"Can't we go?" Carol asked her mother. "Even if we get wet? I'm afraid the lightning will strike here next. This is such a little house."

Carol's father smiled. "It isn't likely," he said. "Many people never see lightning hit anything in their whole lifetime."

"And anyway," Carol's mother added, "we're pretty safe here. The only place that might be safer is the car."

"But the car's even smaller!"

"That's right," said Carol's father. "It's smaller and lower to the ground than the shelter. That's one reason it would be safer.

Lightning nearly always strikes the tallest thing, like the tree that was just hit."

"Why doesn't it strike the short things?"

"Because lightning usually comes down from a cloud to the nearest thing on the ground. A tall tree is nearer to the cloud than a short tree. When you're playing hide-and-go-seek and the one who's it is chasing you, don't you touch home on the spot that's nearest you? Lightning usually does the same thing. It touches the nearest spot."

The room was growing brighter and brighter as the clouds rolled away and the rain stopped. Soon sunlight was shining through the wet window.

Carol's father said, "It looks as if the thunderstorm is touching 'home' somewhere else."

"Before we leave, let's go clean up the table," said Carol's mother.

53

When they got to the table, Carol saw that the cake was very wet.

"Oh, my poor cake—it's just soaked!" Carol turned to her mother. "If you put it back in the oven, will it dry out and get like new?"

"I'm afraid not," answered her mother, "but I'll bake you a new one tomorrow. And we'll stop on the way home and get double ice-cream cones for everybody."

At the drive-in where the children were licking at a rainbow of ice-cream flavors, Carol's father said, "Well, you children have all seen what lightning can do. We're lucky we weren't under that tree when it struck."

54

"I know," Carol said, still thinking of her squishy cake, "but I don't *feel* lucky."

"The rain did spoil your cake," her father said, smiling, "but the lightning lit a really big candle for it—a candle as tall as a tree!"

"You'll be sure to get your wish from a candle as big as that!" one of Carol's friends told her.

"Good!" said Carol, "I wish that a thunderstorm will never come to my birthday party again!"

If you're interested in weather,
read about Rain *in Volume 13*
or Snow *in Volume 14.*

Big Winds

Winds come in all sizes, big and small. Most winds are small. They can be heard when they stir the leaves on a tree or rattle windows. Ordinary winds can cool a person in the summer and make a sailboat move or a windmill turn. Without a wind you could not fly a kite.

Very big winds, however, can be dangerous. The biggest are called cyclones. They are powerful winds that whirl in a circle at great speeds. When a cyclone occurs on the ocean, it is known as a hurricane. In Asia it is sometimes called a typhoon. When a cyclone occurs on land, it is known as a tornado.

56

A hurricane begins near the equator, in the tropical, or warmest, areas of the ocean. Strong winds come together there and begin to whirl in a huge circle. If you could see the winds—which you can't—they would look like a giant wheel. A hurricane's circle of winds may be as much as 500 miles wide. Most hurricanes occur during the period from May through October.

The winds of a hurricane blow at speeds of 75 miles per hour or faster. And a hurricane moves across the ocean at about 10 to 15 miles per hour. It usually moves in a northwest direction.

Inside the winds of a hurricane is an area called the *eye*. In the eye, the winds are light. After a ship passes through the winds of a hurricane into the eye, it will seem to those aboard that the storm is over. But the ship will have to pass through the winds on the other side of the hurricane's circle.

Some hurricanes will die down before they reach land. But those that don't can cause great damage. The winds are strong enough to knock trees down, overturn automobiles, and damage houses. A hurricane also stirs up large waves on the ocean. They can destroy docks and piers, wash away roads, and destroy buildings or houses near the shore. Heavy rainstorms also come with a hurricane. The great downpours can force rivers or streams to overflow and cause floods.

Some of the areas most commonly hit by hurricanes are the United States, especially Florida and the east coast of Texas, Japan, the Philippines, Hawaii, China, India, and Southeast Asia. Some hurricanes have killed thousands of people.

Because hurricanes are dangerous, *meteorologists*, the scientists who study weather, are always on the alert for them. Weather satellites that orbit the Earth take photographs of

cloud formations and the winds and send them back to the scientists on Earth. They can determine if there is a hurricane. They can also tell in what direction and how fast it is moving. Today we will know days ahead that a hurricane is approaching land. People can take measures to protect their property and can protect themselves by moving to safer places.

After a hurricane moves onto land, the circle of winds begins to break up and the winds die down. That is why hurricanes are seldom found very far inland.

Tornados are much smaller than hurricanes. Their whirling winds may only be a few feet wide, but some may be as much as a mile wide. These cyclones, which begin over the land, have winds that may swirl at 300 miles per hour.

Because the winds are so strong, a tornado is the most destructive of any storm. It can knock a train off its track, lift

a house or a truck off the ground, or tear trees out of the earth. An airplane cannot fly through a tornado.

A tornado moves at a speed of from 25 to 40 miles per hour. It can travel in any direction and it usually twists and turns as it goes. It may move along the ground for only a few feet or it may travel as far as 300 miles. Most tornados only last a few minutes.

As you can see from the picture, the whirling winds of the tornado extend down from the clouds. The funnel-shaped cloud spins like a top. What you see is *not* the wind. It is the dirt and debris picked up by the swirling winds and whipped around in a circle. The funnel cloud is often called a *twister*.

Meteorologists constantly study the winds and temperatures so that they can warn people if a tornado is coming. They use photographs from weather satellites and information gathered at weather stations. They can tell when the weather conditions might produce a tornado. Then over radio and television they announce a *tornado watch,* which means that a tornado could develop in a certain area. When a tornado is sighted, a *tornado warning* is broadcast, which tells people where the tornado is and where it is heading.

The announcers on radio and television will tell the people the best ways to protect themselves from a tornado:

—If you are in a house with a basement, go to the basement and stay in the corner nearest the coming tornado.

—If you have a real storm cellar, go to it.

—If you are in the open, run for a ditch or a low place and lie flat.

—If you are in a house with no basement, stay away from windows and doors. Leave a few windows open. This lets the wind blow through the house instead of breaking the windows.

As soon as the danger of a tornado is over, the announcer will let you know it is safe to come out.

What's a Cloud?

Did you ever look up at a soft white cloud and think, "Wouldn't it be fun if I could bounce around on it and lie back in its white softness and take a ride through the sky?"

Have you ever wondered what they are—those big, white, lumpy things moving around in the sky?

Well, what *are* they? You know they're not marshmallows or cotton or soapsuds. But did you know they are *water?* Hundreds and thousands of gallons of water, floating high in the air.

Does that seem hard to believe—that water floats in the air?

Well, it does, even though the water is in such tiny droplets that you couldn't see one even if it were separated from all the others.

It takes billions of tiny droplets to make a big cloud.

Now that you know that clouds are really great clumps of water droplets you can begin to see how clouds bring rain.

Sometimes the water droplets form around tiny pieces of dust in the air.

These droplets with dust in them get bigger and bigger as they join together until they become too heavy to float and they fall— plop!

And that's rain!

But you know that clouds don't *always* bring rain. And clouds don't always look like soapsuds or marshmallows. There are two main kinds of rainy clouds—tall, tall, cottony ones like these on this page.

And flat, gray, dismal-looking ones like these.

The tall, white, cottony rainclouds are called *thunderheads* because they lift their heads so high and they often bring thunderstorms. They also have a big scientific name—*cumulonimbus*. The flat gray ones are called *nimbostratus*.

Besides rain, there are other things that fall from clouds: snow and sleet and hail. Snow and sleet fall only on a cold winter day, but hailstones can fall even on a warm summer day.

Sometimes a cloud is *so* high, where the air is *so* cold, that the whole cloud is made of ice—tiny bright specks of ice floating in the air—instead of tiny drops of water. You can tell these clouds when you see them. They are called *cirrus* clouds and they look like these wispy clouds in the bright blue sky.

If you ride in an airplane, you may get very close to a cloud. You may even go right through one. It's like going through fog. In fact, that's about what a cloud is—fog floating high in the air. Or would you say a fog is just a cloud sitting on the ground?

A cloud can't move by itself. Winds carry clouds through the sky. Sometimes when you don't even feel a breeze, you see the clouds moving. Then you know that winds are blowing high up in the air.

But where do clouds come from, anyway?

When the sun dries up a puddle of water, where does the puddle go? Up!—up into the air. That's where many of the tiny drops of water in a cloud come from—puddles and ponds and rivers and oceans.

So the next time you see a puddle of water on the street, you can say to yourself, "That's going to be part of a cloud." And the next time you see a cloud, you can say, "There's my puddle starting!"

Are you interested in the weather?
Look up Rain *in Volume 13*
and Snow *in Volume 14.*

Watch the Red Thread

Shu-dul-ig! Shu-dul-og!
Shu-dul-ig! Shu-dul-og!
The shuttle flies back and forth, carrying its thread.
Is a shuttle a bird weaving thread into its nest?

No. A shuttle is not a bird at all. A *shuttle* is part of a machine that makes cloth.

The machine is called a *loom*. The shuttle is a small part that has thread inside. *This* shuttle has red thread. When it runs between the rows of blue and black thread, it lays down its own red thread. Then the machine moves the rows of threads past each other. The black threads move up. The blue threads move down. Now they hold the red shuttle thread tightly; and the shuttle goes through again, laying down another thread for them to hold. The shuttle moves swiftly back and forth many, many times each day, making cloth.

Long before there were electric machines to make cloth, people made cloth on handlooms. Sometimes they used their hands to move the shuttle, and their feet pushed pedals to move the rows of thread.

Cloth is made from *fibers*. Fibers by themselves are not of much use; but a long time ago, men learned how to spin the fibers together into long threads.

Where do the fibers come from?

Some fibers come from animals, some from plants. Some even come from an insect! A silkworm. And not long ago, men learned how to *make* fibers. They do this in a special way that seems like magic.

The animal fiber that is used most often to make cloth is wool. Most wool is the hair of sheep, but some comes from other animals, such as goats and camels. Men cut the thick winter wool off the sheep. The clippers that are used are very much like those a barber uses to clip your hair.

Cloth made of wool keeps you nice and warm. That's why wool sweaters, suits, dresses, and socks are usually worn when the weather is cold.

Cotton fibers come from cotton plants. Just before the men pick the cotton, the fluffy balls of cotton make the fields look like fields of snowball bushes.

Cotton cloth can be washed many times without wearing out. It is very strong even when made of thin thread.

Some cotton fibers are so thin that just one pound of them can be spun into a thread 100 miles long!

Work clothes and summer clothes often are made of cotton.

Cloth made out of silk is shiny and smooth. It costs a lot of money. This is because it takes so much work to care for the tiny worms that make silk fibers and also because each worm makes such a small amount of silk.

Silkworms are kept on trays in warm rooms where there are a lot of chopped mulberry leaves for them to eat. The workers are kept busy because silkworms eat all the time, night and day.

How would you like to be a waitress to a worm?

When it is full grown, the silkworm wraps itself in thin silk fibers that come out of its head. This silk wrapping is called a *cocoon,* and it is from this cocoon that silk thread is made.

Men have been making wool, cotton, and silk cloth for a very long time. Both the animal fibers and the plant fibers grow. But the silk fiber doesn't—the silkworm makes it out of juices that are inside its body. Men, too, can make fibers from juices or liquids. Of course, they don't make the fibers inside their bodies like the silkworms. Instead, they use machines.

Be sure to read Thread
in Volume 15.

What Is a Weed?

"Look!" Barbara cried. "Violets! They're growing all over in the grass right in the middle of the yard."

And there they were—purple violets nestled among the blades of green grass. Barbara and Aaron squatted down and started to pick them.

They thought the violets were pretty. You might think so, too. You might even think that yellow dandelions growing in the grass were pretty.

But the man who planted this grass probably wouldn't think so. To him, anything that grows in his grass besides grass is a weed. And weeds soak up some of the water, sunshine, and food that grass needs.

Do you know how to tell which plants are weeds?

If you think a plant is a weed, it *is*.

If you think it isn't a weed, it *isn't*.

Any plant that grows where it isn't wanted is usually called a *weed*.

Farmers grow wheat. People plant roses in their gardens because they like to look at them. But if the farmer found roses in his wheat field, he wouldn't think they were pretty. He would try to get rid of them. The same would be true if the gardener found wheat growing in his rose garden!

A plant is a weed whenever you think it is!

If you liked this story,
look up Flowers *in Volume 6*
and Plants *in Volume 12.*

The Biggest Animal of All

There's something very fishy about whales. They live in the water. They look like fish. They swim like fish.

But they aren't fish at all.

Whales are warm-blooded animals like people and cows and horses. Millions of years ago, their ancestors lived on land. They walked around on four legs and were hairy like other animals.

Then—nobody knows exactly why—they started living more and more in the sea. And finally, they began to look more and more like fish. They lost their hair. And when their bodies became smooth, they could glide through the water easily. Their hind legs also disappeared. They grew a thick layer of fat—called *blubber*—under their skin to keep themselves warm in the cold seas.

With these and a few other changes, they got along very nicely in their watery home.

But because whales are not fish, they can't stay under the water all the time as fish do. They have to come up for air once in a while, or they will drown.

When they come up, the first thing they do is blow out the breath they have been holding. When their warm breath hits the colder air, it makes a cloud of mist, just as our breath does when we blow it while outdoors on a cold day. This mist is called the whale's *spout*.

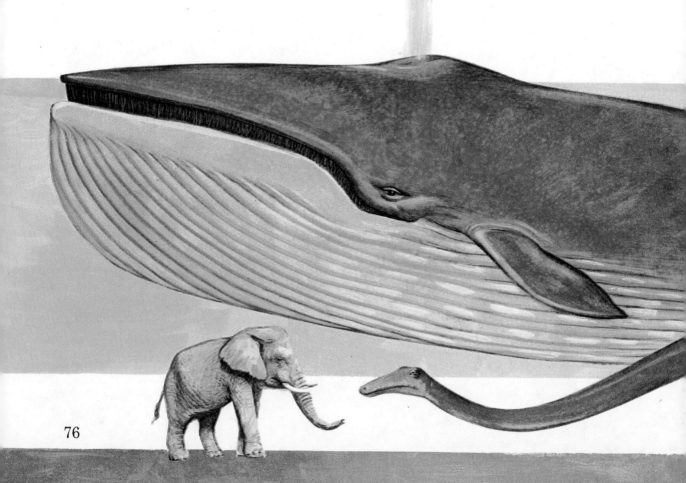

You can spot a whale by its spout.

Sometimes many whales come to the surface and blow at the same time. That is a very fine sight to see.

Another interesting thing happened to whales when they started living in the water. They began to grow bigger and bigger. Some whales are so big now that they couldn't possibly live on land. They would be too heavy to move around. They need the water to hold up part of their great weight.

The biggest whale of all is the blue whale. As far as we know, it is the biggest animal that ever lived. It is much bigger than an elephant. It is bigger than any dinosaur. Even a baby blue whale is a whale of a baby. And the mother whale has to feed it for about six months . . . until it learns to feed itself.

Finding food is a simple matter for blue whales. They just swim along with their huge mouths open, and thousands of tiny sea creatures—some so small that they hardly can be seen—flow in.

Like most of the largest whales, blue whales have no teeth. Instead, they have strings of hardened skin (something like our fingernails) in their mouths. This material is called *baleen,* or *whalebone*. It hangs down in the whale's mouth like a giant comb. The whale can hold thousands of bits of food behind this baleen and strain the salt ocean water out of its mouth.

Most of the smaller whales have teeth. These whales eat fish or any other sea creature they can catch.

One of these smaller whales is the killer whale. (It isn't small compared with other animals. It's small only compared with the giant blue whales.)

The killer whale always has been thought of as a cruel and dangerous animal—the terror of the sea. It eats seals, sea lions, penguins, and even other whales. All fish fear it. Killer whales travel in packs like wolves. They are very fast and strong, and even many sharks are afraid of them. But in recent years a few of the captured killer whales have become good-natured and friendly pets.

Some whales aren't fierce at all. This is especially true of the dolphin, one of the smaller whales. As far back as the ancient days of Greece and Rome, stories were told about dolphins that gave children rides on their backs.

Not many years ago, there was a famous dolphin named Opo who visited the same New Zealand beach almost every day. It played ball with the children in the water and even gave some of them short rides on its back. If one of the big whales would do this, just about everybody in a schoolroom could go for a ride at the same time.

Another dolphin, named Pelorus Jack, used to guide ships safely past the dangerous places in the water in Admiralty Bay, New Zealand.

Now that scientists have begun to study the whole family of whales more carefully, they are amazed at how friendly, playful, and smart many of the whales are. They are learning that whales, like dogs and chimpanzees, can be trained to do many things.

Want to know more?
Look up Dolphins *in Volume 4.*

Before There Were Wheels

Wheels,

wheels,

wheels . . .

Big wheels, little wheels,

wide wheels, thin wheels.

Iron wheels, brass wheels,

and big rubber-tired wheels.

Wheels of wood and wheels of plastic.

Every kind of wheel you can think of—

even toy wheels and candy wheels.

Can you imagine if there weren't any—no wheels anywhere in

the world?

Without wheels many of your toys couldn't move. Your wagon. Your tricycle. Your roller skates.

Without the wheels that go around and around in a factory machine, we couldn't make books or tin cans or any of the other things that are made by machine.

A motorboat couldn't run without the wheels in its engine. An airplane couldn't get off the ground or get safely down again. And a train couldn't run.

Before there were wheels, people did not go very far very fast.

People carried things on their backs or heads or dragged things behind them.

It might be fun to travel this way. But you could go no faster than the people who carried you could walk.

After animals were tamed, things were carried on the backs of camels, llamas, horses, elephants, oxen, and donkeys.

Sometimes two poles were attached to the sides of a horse or a dog. The poles dragged in the dirt behind the walking animal and held the weight of whatever was being moved.

We don't know who was the first one in the world to use a wheel. Perhaps someone watched a log roll down a hill and thought, "What a good way to move something heavy—on top of a rolling log!"

It wasn't a very good way, though. Things kept falling off.

People tried using more than one log and rolling the logs along together. It was hard, slow work, but very heavy weights could be moved in this way.

Try moving a small box—or a brick—in this way— Use a few pencils to carry the weight. Just keep picking up the leftover pencil and placing it in front of the box as you push it along.

Perhaps one day someone cut the end from a log and made the first wheel!

A wheel rolling by itself can't carry anything. The wheel must be attached to something.

The wheel has to be put on a rod called an *axle*. Then the wheel can turn on the axle and make something move. After people found out how to attach a wheel to an axle and attach the axle to a cart or wagon and later to a wheelbarrow or bicycle or train or anything else, life became easier for them.

Today we use so many wheels that it is hard to imagine how people ever got along without them.

You can try it yourself and see how it works. Cut some wheels from stiff paper or cardboard.

Push a pencil through the center of one of the wheels. The pencil is your axle. Wiggle the pencil in the paper to make the hole big enough so that your wheel turns on your pencil axle.

Before you put a wheel on the other end of your axle, bend up the two sides of a piece of cardboard. Push the pencil through the two sides.

Do the same thing with two other wheels and another pencil axle. Now you have a wagon!

Wheels, wheels, wheels . . .
Can you tell what each of
these wheels is?
(The answers are printed upside
down at the bottom of the page.)

*And if you want to know what life was like
before there were* Automobiles, *look in Volume 1.*

1. automobile wheel. 2. airplane wheel.
3. tractor wheel. 4. bicycle wheel.
5. cogwheel of clockworks. 6. a child's
hoop. 7. roller skate wheel. 8. caster
wheel. 9. flanged railroad wheel.
10. Ferris wheel. 11. steering wheel.
12. tricycle wheel. 13. coaster wagon
wheel.

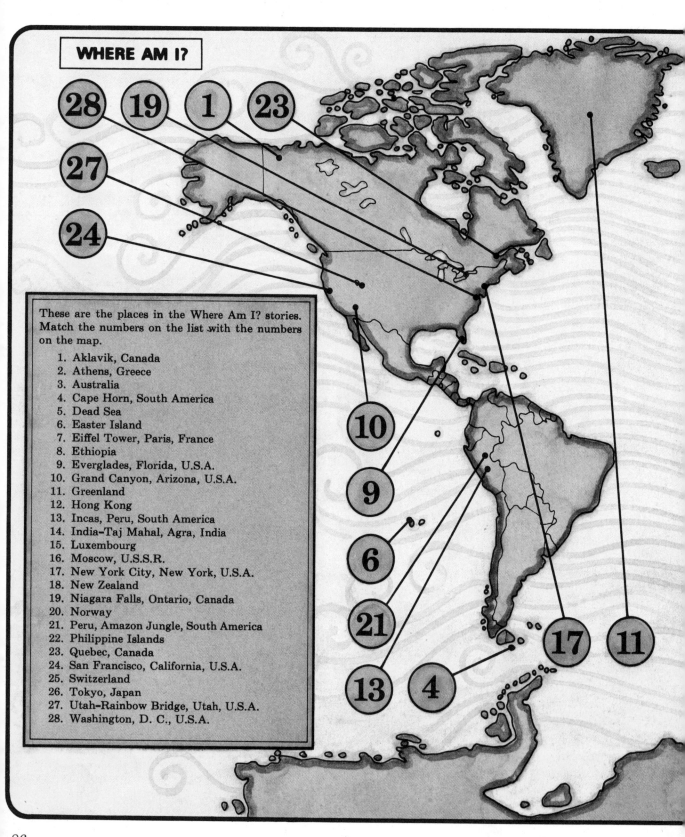

WHERE AM I?

These are the places in the Where Am I? stories. Match the numbers on the list with the numbers on the map.

1. Aklavik, Canada
2. Athens, Greece
3. Australia
4. Cape Horn, South America
5. Dead Sea
6. Easter Island
7. Eiffel Tower, Paris, France
8. Ethiopia
9. Everglades, Florida, U.S.A.
10. Grand Canyon, Arizona, U.S.A.
11. Greenland
12. Hong Kong
13. Incas, Peru, South America
14. India–Taj Mahal, Agra, India
15. Luxembourg
16. Moscow, U.S.S.R.
17. New York City, New York, U.S.A.
18. New Zealand
19. Niagara Falls, Ontario, Canada
20. Norway
21. Peru, Amazon Jungle, South America
22. Philippine Islands
23. Quebec, Canada
24. San Francisco, California, U.S.A.
25. Switzerland
26. Tokyo, Japan
27. Utah–Rainbow Bridge, Utah, U.S.A.
28. Washington, D. C., U.S.A.

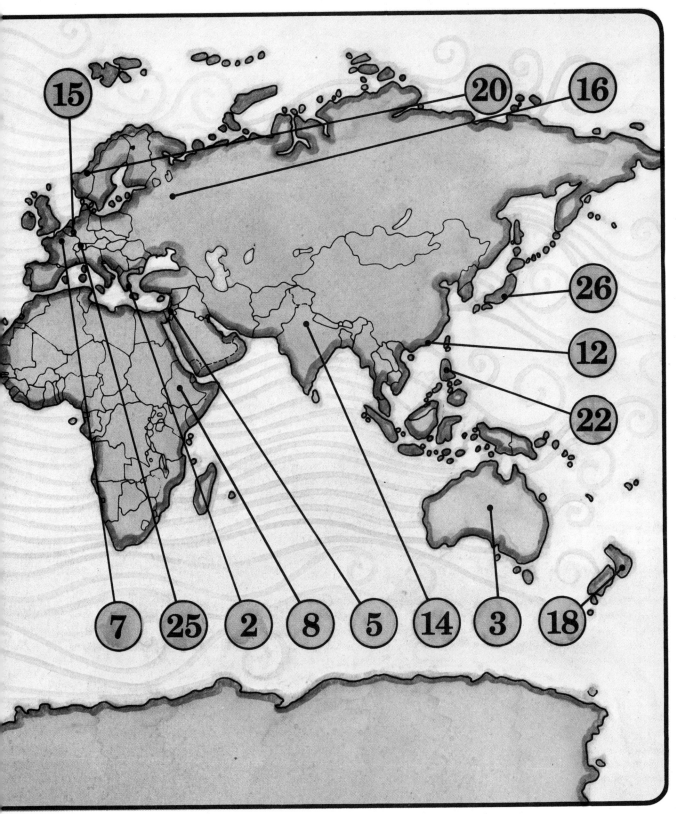

Windmill in Trouble!

One morning Piet awoke to a familiar sound. *Whoosh! Whoosh! Whoosh! Whoosh!*

Piet was a Dutch boy, and he lived in a windmill. The windmill was called Grota Vogel, which means "great bird." Every time one of the great arms of the windmill sailed past Piet's bedroom window, it made a loud whispering *Whoosh! Whoosh!*

The windmill was round and quite high. Its four great arms, which went around and around, were as tall as a house.

Because Grota Vogel was round, Piet's bedroom on the second floor was the shape of a slice of pie. Piet liked to stand at his window and watch Grota Vogel's great arms sweep past.

That day he had a special reason for watching the arms. His parents were going into town. He would be in charge of the windmill while they were gone. Piet dressed and ran downstairs to the kitchen. On the table was a delicious breakfast of hot chocolate, homemade bread, rich Dutch butter, and cheese.

The flat and water-soaked country where Piet lived is called the Netherlands. Sometimes people call it Holland, but that is really just the name of a part of the Netherlands. The land here is lower than the water in the nearby North Sea. Great banks of earth called *dikes* have been built to keep the sea from pushing in and flooding the land.

But it rains a lot in the Netherlands, so windmills are used to pump the water away and keep the land dry enough for farming.

As the great arms of the windmills turn, they cause a wooden wheel with scoops on it to turn also. The water is scooped up from the meadow and pushed into little canals. Other mills push the water in the canals over or through the dikes and into the North Sea.

After breakfast Piet's father said, "The wind is rising. We must get to town and back before the storm breaks." He smiled at Piet. "Be a good boy while we're gone—and take good care of Grota Vogel."

Piet's home was in a large meadow. There were no close neighbors. There were no telephones either. But people had worked out a special way of talking to one another through the windmills. When the windmill's arms were stopped and put in one position, it meant that people were resting. When the arms were in another position, everyone knew the people were not at home. One position meant danger. Another meant that everything was all right.

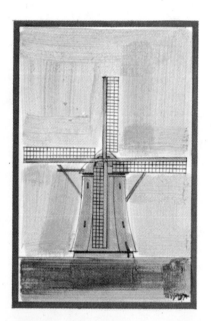

After his parents were gone, Piet went to his room and fell asleep.

Grota Vogel woke him. The great arms of the windmill were sweeping past his window with a moaning sound. He had never seen them move so fast. He hurried to the window and looked out. A high wind was blowing from the sea. The trees were bent, and the meadow grass lay flat.

Piet looked at the other windmills in the distance. They were dead still. Their arms were locked in the position of danger. They were telling him to pull the brake rope and stop the flying arms of Grota Vogel, or the whole mill might be swept away!

As Piet ran out the door, the wind blew against him and knocked him down. But he had to reach the brake rope, which hung down the back of the mill. The brake would stop the mill's arms from spinning. He got up and pushed against the wind, at the same time trying to hold to the side of the mill. He could feel the mill shaking. Would he and the old mill both be swept away?

He tried not to think about it as inch by inch he pushed himself along the trembling side of Grota Vogel. He could see the brake rope whipping in the wind. Three times he grabbed at it and missed. Then the wind scraped the rope across his very face. He grabbed the rope with both hands and pulled with all his might. Slowly the huge arms of the windmill began to stop.

Piet felt as if he had been holding on to that rope forever. But after a while the wind went away. The sky got brighter. The arms of the other windmills were now signaling that all was well.

Then Piet saw his mother and father running toward him. They smiled and waved. As he waited for them, he felt like a very big boy. He had saved Grota Vogel. Behind him the great arms sailed slowly around and around.

Wings
Everywhere

Bird wings
    flap and beat the air, carrying a bird across the sky.
Wings are for diving,
    for gliding,
        for starting,
           for stopping,
              for turning,
                for hovering.
        Insect wings flutter,
          buzz, and hum.
Some flash and glitter in the sun.
Some wings fold like fans.

A little jump, a flap of its
wings—and a chickadee flies.

An airplane has no feathers to
help it fly, and its wings don't flap. Its engines
must speed it along the ground, faster and faster,
before it can go up.

The chickadee keeps flapping its wings and
spreads its feathers to go higher.

The engines of an airplane keep it moving, and its wings take it
high into the air.

When it wants to glide, the chickadee spreads its wings like
sails. Then it can stay in the air without moving its wings.

Airplanes can glide, too, for a while, without the engines
running.

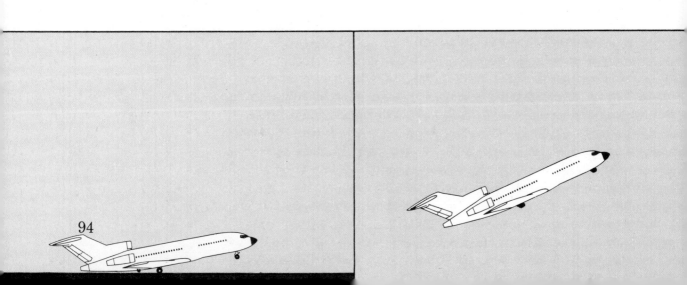

Henry C. Johnson

To make a fast turn, the chickadee lifts one wing and dips the other.

Airplanes do the same thing when they turn.

When the chickadee dives, it tucks its wings so close to its body that it looks like a tiny football going through the air.

When an airplane dives, its wings stay the same way they always were.

In landing, the chickadee spreads its wings and tail to slow itself in the air.

An airplane lowers its flaps to help it land more slowly.

Want to know more?
Read about Airplanes *in Volume 1*
and Kites *in Volume 8.*

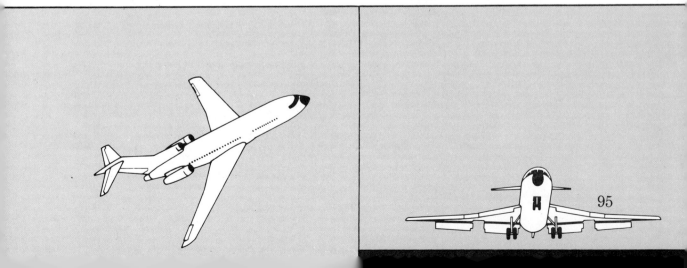

The Takeoff

What has four wheels and flies, although it has no wings?

You probably know the answer—a garbage truck!

Here's another riddle—what is black and white and has two wings but *can't* fly?

If you guessed a penguin, you must have known that not every bird can fly. Most birds do fly, but a penguin is one that can't. It uses its wings to paddle along in the water.

Ostriches can't fly either. But when they run, they spread and flap their wings to help them run faster and to keep from falling over. And ostriches can run faster than the fastest man!

Some birds that fly have trouble getting off the ground and into the air. One of these is the gooney. Before a gooney can fly, it must run along the ground with its wings flapping.

Why does running help? Perhaps it gives the gooney a start into the air. While running, it can jump higher than when standing still. So, faster and faster it waddles and wobbles, gathering speed like an airplane racing down a runway. Sometimes this clumsy bird falls on its beak and must try again.

A loon is another bird that must work hard to get into the air. A loon spends a lot of time in the water, looking for fish to eat. When it wants to fly, it flaps its wings fast to help lift its body partly out of the water and into the air. For a second or two it seems to be running on the water. With a last push of its webbed feet against the water, it rises into the air like a seaplane taking off.

Gliders are like birds in some ways. But a bird can flap its wings while the wings of a glider can't flap. Because of this difference, gliders need help before they can take off. Sometimes a glider is pulled high into the sky by an airplane and then is turned loose to sail back to earth.

Another way to get a glider sailing is to start it from the top of a high hill. A bird named the condor often starts its flight from the top of a hill, too. It can't rise into the air with the ease of a robin because its wings are so long they scrape the ground. So the condor jumps off a high place, flaps its wings, spreads them wide, and soars like a glider.

You may learn about Ostriches *in Volume 11 and* Penguins *in Volume 12.*

Winter in the Country

In winter it's good to see my friends trooping across the white and empty fields in front of my house.

They are wrapped in scarves and topped with caps as brightly colored as summer's prettiest birds. Their boots are as black and shiny as a crow's wing. And the heavy *thump-thump-thump* they make as they cross the porch to our front door is a sound as welcome as the up-and-down trill of a whippoorwill.

There's lots more time to spend with my friends in winter because I don't have so many chores to do around the farm.

The few weeds that are still left are almost too weak to stand. They crumble if I touch them. I almost feel sorry for them. I almost forget the trouble they caused me last summer under the hot sun. All that pulling and tugging when they were green and had as good a grip as I have.

100

The soft black earth of the vegetable garden freezes . . . until it's as hard as a bell. My hoe hangs silently on its hook in the barn like the pendulum of a stopped clock.

Then my friends and I go skating. We skate on the shallow horse pond near the barn. Later—when the creek is frozen— we race down the creek that winds like a country road right through our woods and clear to the next county!

Our farm isn't near any hills for sledding. But we've got a horse that can pull our sled anywhere we want to go.

On days when the weather is just too mean and cold for us to go outdoors, my friends and I keep busy in the house. We scratch our names or make round thimble marks on the thickly frosted windowpanes.

We look at seed catalogs and dream of having real flowers, fruits, and vegetables as perfect looking as those in the pictures.

Sometimes we sit in front of the fire and don't do much of anything. Just being with a good friend on a cold, gray winter day in the country is doing something very important.

Winter in the City

In the winter, city buildings flower with lights. . . .

Now the daytime sky is dull and streaked with smoke. It looks like a blue plate that's been wiped with a dirty cloth. But night comes quickly—and look!

I'm walking through a garden of blue, green, yellow, and rose-colored lights!

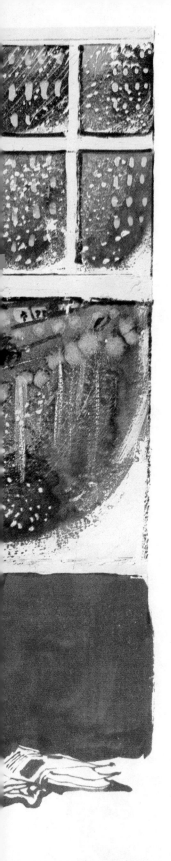

There are other lights in the dark of early morning.

I hurry from our shining white kitchen to the brownish gold gleam of my schoolroom.

In the winter I don't need a ticking clock. I can tell time by the click of the light switch. It's toward noon when my teacher says, "We don't really need all these lights anymore." *Click!*

Looking out the window, long before dinner, I watch the lighted buses go by. They look as bright and happy as circus wagons.

The room where I sleep is very, very dark in winter—except where a soft glow slips in through the sides of the shades. It comes from the still-lighted windows across the street and from the blazing signs that stand on giant stilts away downtown.

The glow in my room is very, very quiet. But I think it has a secret voice. It seems to say, "Go to sleep. Don't be afraid. I will keep watch until the new day."

The Magic Sausage

There was once a hard-working farmer who had a bad-tempered wife who often complained about how poor they were. The two loved each other, though, and usually got along well.

One evening the woman came home before her husband and said to herself, "I'll see what I can find to cook for supper."

There was little to eat, but she could at least boil some soup. She put the kettle on and added a few sticks to the fire.

When her husband came home, he looked at her strangely. Usually he sat down, filled his pipe, and rested for a while before supper. But now he just stared into the fire.

"What in the world is the matter?" his wife asked.

He shook his head slowly. "You would have to try for a long time, wife, before you could guess what happened to me today."

"Then tell me right away."

"You won't believe me."

"Tell me anyway and see whether I do."

"Well, I was walking home through a cornfield, and it was nearly dark. I saw something moving far off at the edge of the road. So I went over to see what it was."

"Tell me. Tell me, what was it?"

"I almost ran when I saw it. I thought it was an evil fairy. But I heard a soft voice call, and I went closer."

The farmer's wife stirred impatiently.

"Yes, yes! What was it?"

"I'm telling you. Wait until I get the words out. The thing I saw was a tiny coach, no bigger than my boot. It had four wheels and looked like a wagon with a roof. Only it was much prettier. It was pulled by four horses. Each horse was so small I could have held it in my hand. Inside the coach was the tiniest old lady you can imagine, all dressed in gold."

"I think you're fooling me," the farmer's wife said. Since her husband's story sounded so silly, she was beginning to lose her temper.

But he went on, "It was the lady's voice I had heard. She begged me to help her get her coach out of the muddy ditch.

"And I suppose you stayed and helped her?"

"At first I was doubtful," he answered, "but after all, she was an old lady, so I couldn't say no. I lifted the horses and coach out of the ditch and put them down on solid ground. Then the little old lady started asking me questions."

"What kind of questions?"

"She asked whether I was married. I said I was. She asked whether we were rich. I said we were the two poorest people in our village. She said *that* could be fixed."

"Hah! And just how did she plan to fix it?"

"She said she would give my wife three wishes, any three wishes. Then she just disappeared—coach, horses, and all!"

The wife laughed. "You had a dream, that's all. If you would stay awake and work harder instead of sleeping and dreaming about little old ladies, maybe we'd have more to eat than soup!"

"You don't know whether or not it was a dream," her husband said. "Think of something you want and make a wish."

"Oh, I suppose I might as well show you that you were just dreaming. Let's see." She looked into the fire, which was now burning brightly. "I wish we had a fine big sausage cooking for supper on this good fire."

She had hardly finished saying this when down the chimney came a great frying pan, and in it was the longest, fattest sausage either of them had ever seen.

"This is wonderful!" they both said together.

"But we must be more careful with our next two wishes," the husband said. "If we wish wisely, we can be rich. Then the first thing I'll do is go to market and buy two horses and a new plow and two young cows and a suckling pig——"

He filled his pipe and leaned over to get a coal from the fire to light it with. But he was so clumsy that he knocked over the frying pan. The sausage fell into the fire and started to burn.

"Oh! Oh!" shouted the wife. "Our beautiful sausage! Look what you've done, you clumsy man! I wish that sausage would grow right onto your stupid nose!"

The moment she said this, the sausage jumped out of the fire. It stuck to the husband's nose and hung almost to the floor.

"You call me stupid?" shouted the husband. "Now look how you've wasted our second wish! Come on, help me get this thing off."

"Hold still, and I'll pull."

His wife pulled gently. Then she pulled hard. But the harder she pulled, the more her husband cried, "Ouch! Help! Stop! You're pulling my nose off!"

Then they just sat and looked at each other with great unhappiness.

"How about cutting it off?" asked the wife after a while.

"Can't you see that this sausage has become part of me?" her husband shouted. "Would you cut off my arm or my leg?"

"Of course not." She thought for a time. "It doesn't look too bad. I don't suppose you'd want it just to stay there?"

"What!" shouted the husband. "Can you see me plowing with this thing on my face? And what would the neighbors say? And how could you ever kiss me again with this sausage in the way?"

"I guess that's not such a good idea after all," said the wife. "Well, what do you think we should do?"

"You know what we should do. You have one wish left."

"But what about getting rich—and the horses and the plow and the cows and the pig?"

"We may never get them," said the husband. "But I can't walk around the rest of my life with a sausage on my nose!"

They argued for a long time. Finally, the wife said she would wish the sausage back into the frying pan. She did, and the sausage flew off the farmer's nose back into the frying pan. But now the three wishes were all used up, and the farmer and his wife were as poor as ever.

They did have a good meal of sausage that night, though. Afterwards, they talked. They knew that because of their tempers and their arguing, they had wasted the three wishes. The man and his wife decided they wouldn't argue anymore.

They got along better together and better in the world. They worked hard and saved their money. Soon they were able to buy the horses and the plow and the cows and the suckling pig. They didn't need any wishes. The farmer and his wife were happy without them. And the farmer was extra happy not to have a sausage on his nose.

How Do You Tell a Storybook Wolf from

Let's look at what the storybook wolf did in the story of Little Red Riding Hood.

Remember the story? Little Red Riding Hood was taking a basket of food to her grandmother who lay sick in bed in her little house deep in the woods. On her way, Little Red Riding Hood met a wolf who asked her where she was going.

Now Little Red Riding Hood's mother had told her not to talk to anybody along the way. But she forgot and told the wolf where her grandmother lived and that she was sick in bed. . . .

You don't have to know much about wolves to know that they do not speak or understand words.

But do you know that wolves can't make plans the way people do? Wolves don't say to themselves, "First I will do this. Then I will do that. And then I will do that." Wolves don't seem to think very much about anything. They do feel many things—hunger, cold, fear. . . .

The minute wolves feel one of these things, they usually do something about it. A hungry, real wolf that met a little girl alone in the woods might eat her right on the spot!

When the wolf heard that Little Red Riding Hood's grand-mother lay sick and helpless in bed, he ran ahead as fast as he could to her house. He tied up Little Red Riding Hood's grand-mother and locked her in the closet. Then he pushed a nightcap down over his ears and crawled into bed. . . .

14

No real wolf puts on people's clothing to fool the creatures it is trying to catch. But the color of some wolves at different times of the year protects them from enemies and helps them sneak up and catch the animals they eat.

In spring and summer, when baby wolves are born, the fur of the wolf is reddish brown. This is the color of the ditches and shallow open caves where a wolf family makes its home.

In winter the coat of a wolf turns yellowish brown like the dead leaves and weeds in the woods where it lives.

The fur of the Far North wolf turns snowy white and darkens only after the long winter is over.

Little Red Riding Hood went right into her grandmother's bedroom and sat down beside the bed.

"How nice to see you, my dear," said the storybook wolf, trying to make his gruff voice as sweet as the grandmother's.

Little Red Riding Hood looked at her grandmother's bedcap, which the wolf's stiff ears kept poking up higher and higher. "What big ears you have," she said.

"The better to hear you with, my dear," said the wolf.

Then Little Red Riding Hood looked at her grandmother's eyes. "What big eyes you have, Grandmother."

"The better to see you with, my dear," said the wolf, smiling.

Little Red Riding Hood looked at her grandmother's smile. "And what big teeth you have, Grandmother!"

"The better to eat you with!" cried the wolf, jumping out of bed.

When Little Red Riding Hood heard *that*, she turned and ran. She ran until she came to some woodchoppers who were working in the forest. When she told them what had happened, they went back to the little house and killed the wolf with their axes. . . .

Most wolves can run faster than foxes and even deer. So a real wolf could easily have caught Little Red Riding Hood.

But the storybook wolf and the real wolf are alike in one way. They both want to eat living things. Real wolves can't live on grass and leaves and the roots of plants as some animals do. They have to eat meat. If they don't, they get sick and die. This is the way wolves are. It is not because wolves are mean or bad.

A hundred years ago, there were more wolves than wolf food. There just weren't enough wild animals for the wolves to kill and eat. Hungry wolves came out from their natural homes—the deep forests—and killed farm animals, such as sheep and cows and horses. So the farmers started killing the wolves. They killed so many that now there are not many wolves left.

But wolves are still bad in most stories. It doesn't hurt their feelings, though. That's because wolves can't read.

If you want to read about other wild animals, read "Animals at Home" under Nature *in Volume 11.*

117

WOOD

The Boy Who Couldn't Get Away from Trees

It would be
nice to be
as useful as a tree.

Trees are beautiful to look at, don't you think?
And, on hot summer days, it's nice to play in
the shade of a tree where it's just a little bit
cooler.

When the wind blows and the tree's leaves rub
together, it's nice to listen to the soft, rustling
sound.

Here is a story to show just how useful trees
are. In this story all the things that Johnny sees
or uses that are made from wood or that come
from trees are *printed like this*.

"Johnny, it's time to get up!" called Johnny's mother.

"Can't I stay in *bed* just a little bit longer?" Johnny called back.

"If you do, your hot *chocolate* will get cold."

Johnny liked hot *chocolate*, so he quickly got dressed. He wondered if there would be pancakes and *maple syrup* for breakfast.

As Johnny pulled his *chair* up to the *table*, he saw that his breakfast was going to be hot oatmeal with *dates* on top. That was fine with him. He liked all kinds of fruit—*peaches, cherries, pears, apples, oranges, figs,* and *grapefruit.*

The day was cold. The sun was dim. Johnny wondered if there would be snow, so he could slide on the *sled* he had found under the *Christmas tree* last year.

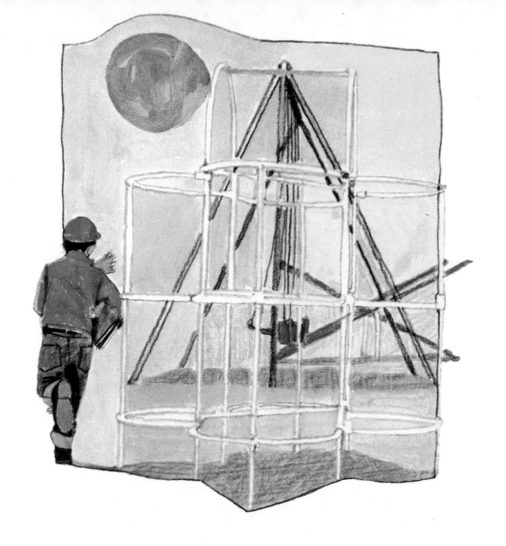

"Johnny, what are you doing leaning against the *windowsill?* It's time for you to leave for school." Johnny's mother was standing near the front *door,* holding his coat and cap and gloves.

"Oh, I almost forgot my *book!*" Johnny clattered up and then down the *stairs.* He ran down the walk, not even stopping to close the *gate* in the *fence.* He was afraid he would be late for school.

As he ran by the school playground, he saw that it was empty. The *teeter-totters* and *swings* looked lonely. He must be late! The other children must all be inside at their *desks.* He'd better hurry, hurry, hurry.

"Hello, Johnny! Where's the fire?"

Mr. Tower, the school janitor, leaned against his broom *handle*. He had been sweeping the *floor* of the long hall, stopping once in a while to reach into a box and throw down some clean *sawdust*. The *sawdust* had a prickly smell, and made the *floor* shine as if it had specks of gold in it.

"I must be early!" Johnny said.

"Mr. Tower nodded. "You're the first boy I've seen today. How would you like to help me run the flag up the *flagpole?*"

Johnny was so afraid that Mr. Tower would change his mind that he quickly nodded his head about ten times and didn't say a word.

On his way home from school, Johnny thought about all the nice things that had happened to him that day. Besides Mr. Tower's letting him help with the flag, his teacher had sent him—all by himself—to the supply room to get a *box* of *pencils* and a *box* of *rubber bands*. After that, he made the highest grade in the class on his spelling *paper*. Then, at recess, because it was so cold outside, his class got to play in the gym. They had races on the gym *floor*, climbed on the *bars*, and swung on the *trapeze*. And some of the older girls played the *piano*.

"Hi, Johnny! Why are you wearing that great big smile?"

Johnny looked around his yard. He couldn't see where the voice came from. All he could see was a squirrel holding a *nut*.

Suddenly Mr. Lemke, the man who lived next door to Johnny, rose up from behind a *cart* piled high with fallen *leaves*.

"I'm over here," he said. "I'm putting *leaves* on my flower beds to keep the plants warm in this cold weather."

Johnny picked up an empty *basket* and bent to lift the rake *handle* from the ground. "I'll rake some more *leaves,* Mr. Lemke."

A folded *newspaper* flew past Johnny's head and landed on Mr. Lemke's front *porch* near the *door.* Johnny knew without even looking that Pat, the afternoon paper boy, had thrown it. Pat was a good baseball pitcher. Tossing *newspapers* was one of the ways he practiced. He was good with a *bat,* too.

"Look at that!" said Mr. Lemke.

"You mean the way Pat can aim a *newspaper?*" asked Johnny.

"No, the snow! It's starting to snow. I'd better hurry and get this *cart* into the *garage.*"

"And I'd better hurry home and find my *sled,*" Johnny said.

Wood was burning cheerily in the fireplace when Johnny went into the *house.* For an after-school snack he popped corn over the *wood coals* and roasted *chestnuts.* He went to sleep that night with a happy feeling about his day. When he was a little older, he would know how trees had helped make it a good day.

To learn more, look under
Trees *in Volume 15.*

Rat-a-tat-tat, What Bird Is That?

Rat-a-tat-tat!
What bird is that?
Rat-a-tat-tat!
It woke up the cat!

It pecks and pecks
And *pecks* all day.
I wish that bird
Would fly away.

Why does a woodpecker pick wood—instead of soft, cool grass or leaves—to peck on?

Because it likes to eat the insects that chew their way into the bark of trees.

Woodpeckers help protect trees against insects that are eating away inside the bark. Woodpeckers have long, hard beaks, which can *rat-a-tat-tat* through wood without breaking. The woodpecker's tongue is extra long and shaped like a spear. After the bird has pecked through the bark, it flicks out its tongue and spears the insect or its eggs for dinner.

The woodpecker has four long, strong toes on each foot—two in front and two in back. Each toe has long, strong claws, which keep the bird from slipping while it is chipping.

The stiff, pointed tail feathers help, too. The woodpecker presses them hard against the tree to keep from falling.

Woodpeckers also use their long, hard beaks to build their homes. They peck big round holes, usually in dead trees, and make their nests inside.

The nests are so comfortable and provide such safe shelter that other birds often move into them after the woodpecker has moved out. The woodpecker builds a new home every year.

Among all the birds, the woodpecker is the best carpenter.

If you liked this story, read Birds *in Volume 2.*

Falling Buildings!

On the day this beautiful building first opened, the band played and everyone cheered. The mayor was there to cut the ribbon. This meant that the new building was open to the public —that people could go inside.

Everyone was anxious to go to the top floor and look out of the windows, because this new building was the tallest in town—five stories high! They all wanted to see the city spread out beneath them—what a wonderful view!

Mr. Barnes, who owned the building, was very proud and happy. A few of the offices were already rented, and now that the building was officially open, he was certain he would quickly rent the rest.

As time passed the city grew up around the building. New buildings were built, using new ideas. Some of these buildings were very tall, some had large windows, some had a different kind of lighting.

When Mr. Barnes's son took over his father's business he put elevators and new lighting into the building. But buildings wear out just as other things do.

By the time Mr. Barnes's grandson owned the building the city had grown. It had become so crowded that there was no land left for any new buildings to be built on. The only place to grow was up!

Young Mr. Barnes decided to knock down his grandfather's old building and build the newest one in town, just as his grandfather had done. The new building would hold many more offices than there were in the old one.

The men who knock down buildings—they are called *wreckers*—
have to do their work carefully to keep from damaging nearby
buildings or automobiles, or hurting people that pass by.

Before any wrecking can begin, the engineers look at the plans
of the building to see how it was built and what is inside the floors
and walls. When they know this, they can tell what kinds of tools
they will need to use in wrecking the building. And they can tell
what parts of the building may be worth trying to save to use
again.

128

The wreckers put up a fence around the building. In some cases this is a colorful fence made of doors removed from the building before the wrecking starts. The fence is meant to keep everyone but the workers outside. If there is a sidewalk in front of the building, the workers block it off or cover it with a heavy roof that people can walk under safely.

The electricity, gas, and water have to be shut off, and then the wrecking can begin.

Some small buildings are made almost completely out of wood. The wreckers usually tear this kind of building down with crowbars. The men pry the boards apart and save some of the lumber.

Larger buildings made of brick, stone, or steel are knocked apart with a large metal ball or pulled apart by a two-jawed scoop called a *clamshell*.

Wrecking is a noisy business. The metal ball swings at the end of a long wire rope, or cable. The crane operator moves the long beam attached to the high mast, called a boom, that guides the metal ball swinging at the end of the cable. The ball smashes against walls, beams, or whatever part of the building the operator is knocking down. Sometimes he just lifts the ball and lets it fall —*bang!*—onto roofs or floors to break them apart.

When a large wall falls it shakes the earth and makes a loud roar.

Often it may be easier and safer to pull a beam down or a wall apart than to knock it down. Then the clamshell may be used.

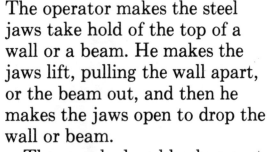

The operator makes the steel jaws take hold of the top of a wall or a beam. He makes the jaws lift, pulling the wall apart, or the beam out, and then he makes the jaws open to drop the wall or beam.

The smashed and broken parts of the wrecked buildings are loaded by *bulldozers* into trucks. (Bulldozers, which usually clear land and move soil and rocks, can also scoop up the broken parts of the building to load the trucks.) The trucks then go to the dump. If any of the boards or bricks are not broken they may be saved and sold.

Once the ground is cleared, the builders can come in. Soon the new building will start to go up, and then one day—a party to celebrate a new opening.

Want to know more?
Look up Buildings *in Volume 2*
and Hands *in Volume 7.*

A Famous King Makes a Mistake

High on a mountain, Xerxes, king of Persia, looked down on the waters of Salamis where hundreds of great Persian warships were fighting the small Greek Navy. Xerxes wanted to be as great as his father, King Darius, and conquer other lands.

"I will be king of all countries—the king of kings!" Xerxes had boasted.

And so he made a bridge of boats for his army to march across. His soldiers chopped through a mountain that stood in their way. Xerxes himself beat the ocean with a whip because, as he said, it dared to sink some of *his* ships in a storm!

His huge army marched through Greece and easily won battle after battle. Now, sure of winning the last one, King Xerxes leaned back on his throne to watch his ships fighting.

Below, the warships banged and rammed each other . . . until the sea was filled with sinking ships and drowning men. Fires broke out. Through the smoke-filled air, a tired messenger climbed the mountain. Xerxes waited to hear the messenger say that the battle had been won. Instead, the messenger cried out, "The Greeks have won! Those are the ships of Persia sinking!"

Proud Xerxes could not believe the news. How could he be beaten by those small Greek boats? But it was true. Xerxes' ships were too big, and there were too many. There was not room enough for them to move around in the small bay. The small Greek ships moved fast and sank them.

Xerxes fled back to Persia with what was left of his navy and his big army. He never fought the Greeks again.

You may read about another
Greek battle in "The Trojan Horse"
under Greeks *in Volume 7.*

A Very Special Picture

Timmy was a little nervous when he went to the hospital after he fell. His arm hurt, and Dr. Zimm was going to X-ray it.

In the X-ray room, a nurse smiled and asked Timmy to sit in a chair and rest his hurt arm on a table. Then she went over to a big machine.

"Is that going to hurt?" Timmy asked.

When the nurse said it wouldn't, Timmy felt better.

"It's only going to take a picture of the bones in your arm," she said.

"Right through my skin?"

"Yes," she nodded. "X rays," she told Timmy, "can take a picture—a shadow picture—through cloth, leather, wood—even through metal."

"Are they magic?" Timmy asked.

Dr. Zimm had come in, and he said, "No, they're not magic, Timmy. But they *are* very powerful and *can* be dangerous if not used carefully."

The doctor explained that the nurse's apron and gloves were made of rubber mixed with lead, and that this protected her when she worked around the X-ray machine.

"Lead is one thing X rays *can't* go through," the doctor said.

"Will the X rays make my arm better?" Timmy asked.

"No, but the picture will show whether a bone is broken," the doctor said. "If it is, I'll know how to fix it."

The doctor also explained that if someone swallows a pin or a penny, an X-ray picture will show where it is stuck. He said that doctors who take care of pets also use X rays to find out what is wrong with a sick animal. Even tree doctors use X rays when trees aren't healthy. And dentists take X-ray pictures of teeth to find out whether there are any hidden cavities.

"Do only doctors and nurses use X rays?" Timmy asked.

The doctor said no, that in factories some workers use X rays to check the parts of automobiles, airplanes, radios, and many other things.

Then he told Timmy, "We could go into an old building with X rays and find out whether there are pipes and wires behind the walls."

Timmy grew excited. "Or maybe hidden treasure!"

The doctor laughed. "Sure, if there's any there."

"When did X rays ever get started?" Timmy wanted to know. The doctor told him that long ago a man named Wilhelm Roentgen was experimenting with electricity—that means he was trying to do new things with it. While he was running the electricity through a glass tube in which there was a tiny bit of a special gas, he saw a strange glow of light on a screen nearby. When he put his hand between the tube and the screen, he could see the bones of his hand in a shadow picture on the screen. He didn't know what the strange light was. He called it *X rays*. Later, his discovery made him famous and won prizes for him.

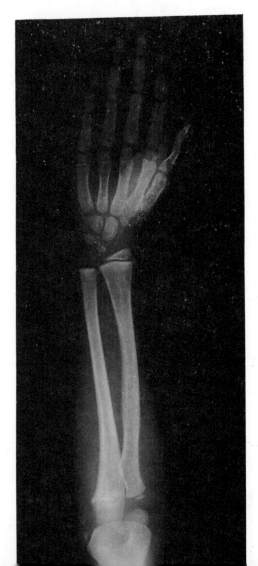

When Dr. Zimm looked at the X-ray picture of Timmy's hand, he said, "No broken bones, Timmy. Only a bad bruise. You'll be fine in no time at all."

You may read about
Doctors *and* Dentists *in Volume 4.*

Growing Up

When I was small, to open doors
   I had to stand on tippy-toes
And pull the doorknob with both hands;
   Then scoot before the door could close.

But now doorknobs are shoulder high.
   I open doors quick as a wink
With just one hand (and no tiptoes).
   I must have grown, 'cause doors don't shrink.

In the first months of our lives, our bodies grow very fast—
faster than they ever will again. The people who study growing
tell us that we begin to slow down after the first few months. We
keep on growing but s-l-o-w-l-y until we are about ten years old.

Then most of us start growing fast again. To the end of our teen
years, we go up, up, up! (But we do not all grow the same amount
at the same time. Some of us start later and continue to grow for
a longer time.)

At the beginning of our 20's, most of us stop growing.

It's a good thing we do. If we didn't, we'd have to build new
houses and cars every year or so.

136

And it's a good thing, too, that our minds need never stop growing. We can keep learning new things as long as we live.

For a long time, people thought there was little they could do about the way things grow. Then some professors and doctors began to study plants and animals. Later they studied how people grow.

There is still much to learn about how and why people grow, but we do know a little right now.

We know that if the grown-ups in our families are tall, we, too, are likely to be tall.

We know that the kind of food we eat has something to do with how well our bones and muscles grow and how healthy we are.

137

How We Know the World Around Us

138

Look at these doll children in their beautiful clothes.

Their eyes are wide and bright. Their ears are as pretty as sea-shells. They have cute little noses and smiling mouths. Their hands are as graceful as a dancer's.

But their eyes,
> ears,
>> noses,
>>> mouths,
>>>> and hands
>>>>> are just pretend.

Yours work!

Your eyes are like cameras—if cameras could work much, much faster than they do and could keep working all the time.

All day, everywhere you look, your eyes are making pictures for you to see.

When you take pictures with a camera, you can paste them in a photograph album to keep them.

Under each picture you can write something about the picture.

My best friend.

My favorite aunt, at Christmastime.

The seashore where I found sea-shells during vacation.

The pictures your eyes take are kept in part of your brain and are part of your *memory*.

While your eyes are sending pictures to one part of your brain, your ears are sending messages to another part.

Your ears hear a sound.

Your brain goes to work.

Grr-rr-rr-rr goes the sound that your ears send to your brain.

"That sounds like a big bear growling," thinks your brain. "But there are no bears around here. I'd better think some more before I decide what it is."

So your brain thinks about the sound your ears have received. And then it knows for sure. "Why, it's just an old car that's stuck in the mud!"

Your nose sends other messages to your brain. You know when something smells good or bad—or dangerous, like smoke.

Your tongue is another messenger.

And any part of you that is touched or touches tells you something.

We use our eyes, ears, noses, tongues, and the rest of our bodies to help us find out more about the world around us.

Are you interested in the senses?
Look under Eyes and Ears *in Volume 5.*

Hiccups

I think there's nothing—*hic!*—so bad
    As—*hic!*—cups that you cannot stop.
They start so suddenly. They—*hic!*—
    They make your—*hic!*—words jump and hop.

Sometimes they're quick like *hic! hic! hic!*
    Sometimes they're slow—you think they're through.
Then, when you don't expect—*hic!*—them,
    Another—*hic!*—comes out of you.

Your aunt will tell you, "Hold your breath
    And count to ten—but very slow.
Now are they gone?" You're not quite sure;
    You'll have to wait and see—*hic!*—No.

Your Uncle Pete says, "Bow your head
    And drink some water upside down."
But that gets water in your nose
    And—*hic!*—it makes you sneeze and frown.

Your friends all tell you things to do;
    Each one of them has got a trick.
You try them all but nothing works;
    You keep—*hic!*—cupping—*hic! hic! hic!*

You—*hic!*— for hours—and as you do,
    Your body shakes from toe to top.
And then as quickly as they came,
    With one last—*hic!*—your hiccups stop.

142

143

How We Move

Inside our skin there are bones. Our fingers can feel them almost everywhere. One bone is attached to another, and when the bones move, we move.

But our bones cannot move themselves.

Our *muscles* move them.

Our bones are covered with muscles. The muscles move them in many directions. That is the job of muscles—to move things.

How do our muscles move our bones?

Our muscles move our bones by pulling them. Muscles always pull—they never push.

144

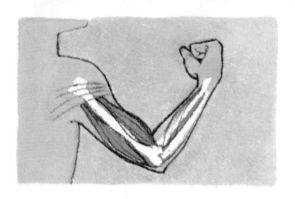

The pink muscle is doing the pulling to bend the arm.

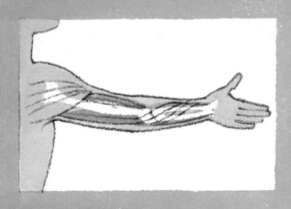

Now a different muscle is pulling to straighten the arm.

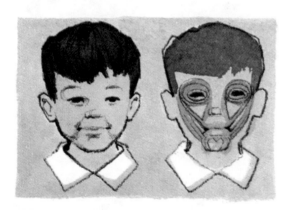

We can feel the jaw muscles in our cheeks become hard as they pull our jaw closed when we bite.

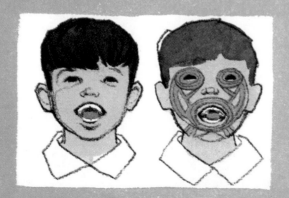

We can feel the muscle under our jaw pull to open our mouth wide.

145

Some muscles don't move
bones. They move *other* things.

Our heart is the muscle that
pumps the blood. To understand
how it works, imagine a few
children standing in a circle with
their arms hooked together. If
they all *pull* at the same time,
what happens?

They squeeze the circle smaller.

When the heart squeezes like
this, the blood is pumped out
and through the body.

146

Tiny muscles move our eyes up, down, and from side to side.

The muscles of our mouth, lips, and face move to make us smile or frown.

Without muscles the skin would be like a bag. And a man would be a bag of bones!

Using Your Head

I think about the reason why
The sun and moon are in the sky
And how the tears drip from my eye
And how a kite can fly so high.

I think about the reason for
The seeds inside an apple core
And how the waves get to the shore
And how a lion roars its roar.

Did you ever stop to think about *why* you can think? Or *how* you think? Or how important it is to think?

Long ago, cavemen learned to make sparks by hitting two special rocks together. These sparks made fire. When the fire spread to the forest and burned the things the cavemen needed for food, they learned that they had to be careful with fire. They also learned that fire does not burn water, so they used the water to put out small fires. And they learned to hide in the water during large fires.

After the cavemen taught their children how to make fire, the children knew something that had taken their parents years to learn. The children then had time to learn new things and time to find out better ways to do old things. Soon they knew more than their parents did—because they knew the things their parents had taught them, and they knew the things they had figured out for themselves.

When someone says, "Use your head," he really means, "Use your brain." Your brain is inside your head.

Your brain does many different things. One thing it does is to find out what's happening outside your body and what the things outside your body are like.

To do this the brain depends on your eyes, ears, nose, tongue, and skin. These helpers send messages to the brain through many thin, stringlike things called *nerves*.

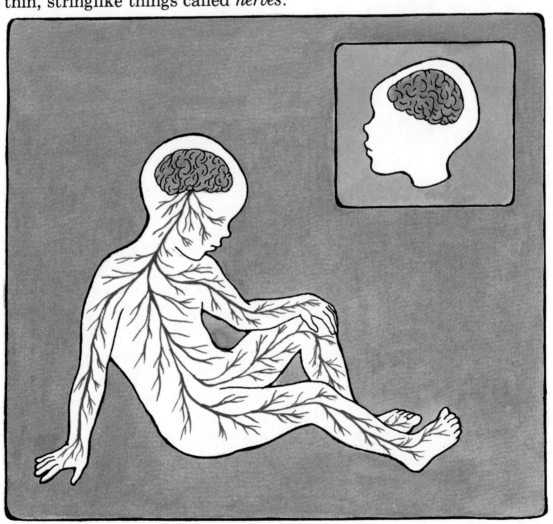

If your mother gives you a bowl of fresh strawberries, your eyes see the plump red berries and your nose smells the good strawberry smell. These messages go to your brain through the nerves, and you know that there are strawberries for you to eat.

When you spoon some of the berries into your mouth, your tongue sends a message to the brain about the delicious taste. The skin in your mouth sends a message about how good the juicy strawberries feel between your teeth and your tongue. Your ears send a message about the sound of your spoon scraping in the bowl.

Another thing the brain does is to make the parts of the body move. When your mother sets the bowl of strawberries in front of you, your brain gets the message from your eyes and nose.

Then the brain makes the muscles in your arm and hand work to pick up your spoon, scoop up some strawberries, put them into your mouth, and take the spoon out again.

Then your brain makes the muscles in your jaw move to chew and makes those in your throat move to swallow.

To move your muscles the brain sends messages through other nerves. These nerves go to every muscle in your body.

Think of all the things you see, hear, smell, taste, feel, and do each day. What a busy brain you have!

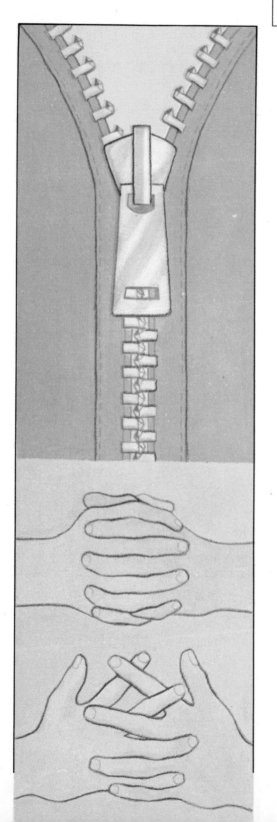

How Do They Work?

Can you hook your fingers together? See—that's the way a zipper works. It's hard to pull your hands apart when your fingers are hooked together. Your zipper holds together in the same way.

Now unhook one pair of fingers. Your hands start to come apart. That's how a zipper opens.

Let's look closely at a zipper. All along each side of the zipper are little "fingers" clamped to a tape. On the top of each finger is a little bump that fits into a hollow at the bottom of the opposite finger.

Zip! Zip! You zip the zippers. Your boots are closed—or your snowsuit. It's almost like magic.

What "magic" thing fits the zipper bumps into the hollows? A slide that goes up the middle of the zipper, guiding the bump of one finger into the hollow of the other. That's how the zipper closes.

When the slide goes down the middle, separating every bump from its hollow, the zipper opens.

When your grandparents were children, zippers were not yet widely used. Then how did jackets and boots and dresses fasten together? With buckles, buttons, hooks, and snaps. About 70 years ago, people with new ideas thought up better ways to fasten things. The zipper, or slide fastener, was invented. And ever since, people have been finding ways to make better zippers— and more uses for zippers.

Zippers for sleeping bags,
   Zippers for suits,
Zippers for purses,
   And zippers for boots.

*If you liked this story,
you'll like* Buttons *in Volume 2
and* Clothes *in Volume 3.*

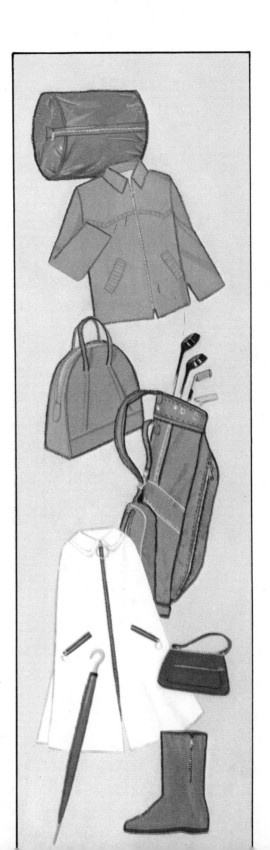

A Good Place for Animals to Live

Look closely at this picture. What do you see?

Three small children with nowhere to hide . . . and running toward them—lions!

How can the children get away from the lions? What will they do?

The children don't have to do anything. They don't have to run from the lions. They can stay right where they are. The lions can't get them.

Why can't they? Because the lions are in a zoo.

154

It isn't the kind of zoo where the lions have to stay in cages. It's a zoo that was built to look like the lion country in Africa. Look closely again at the picture.

Hidden below the bushes is a deep ditch filled with water. It is too wide for the lions to jump across. This ditch, called a *moat,* keeps people safe from the lions. (It also keeps the lions safe from people!)

Zoos like this one are good for both animals and people. The animals are free to run around in the open area. At the same time, people have a chance to watch wild animals behaving as they might in the jungles or grassy plains where they were born.

Lions aren't the only animals that we can see in this way. Zebras, giraffes, deer, buffalo, and many other animals that like to run are given plenty of room in this kind of zoo.

Not all animals can be given this much freedom. Leopards are such good jumpers that they have to be kept in cages. And you might guess that snakes are good at crawling over, under, through, or around almost anything. In a zoo, snakes live in glass cages, and birds live in big wire cages.

People always have liked to look at wild animals when it was safe to do so, and to see to it that captured animals are kept healthy and comfortable. Zoo keepers try to know everything they can about the habits of the animals in their care: what foods they eat, how warm or how cold their living places should be, what vitamins and medicines they need—even what friends they need.

There was an elephant in one zoo that became very unhappy
unless a little Shetland pony stayed with it. The pony seemed to
be the elephant's pet!

And zoo keepers have found that monkeys like people. Monkeys
like to watch the people while the people watch them.

Have you ever seen a monkey mountain? Hundreds of monkeys running up and down and jumping and playing on a "mountain" of rocks and dirt? They can't get away because there is water all around the mountain, and these monkeys don't like to get wet.

What do you think happens when a hippopotamus in a zoo gets a toothache? That's right. The hippo goes to a dentist. And when animals get sick, they go to the zoo hospital. Zoos even have nurseries where baby animals can stay when they need special care.

Lions and tigers are meat eaters. Zebras and camels and elephants eat plants. The eucalyptus leaves that koala bears eat can be grown only in a few places in the world. So even though these furry roly-poly creatures are friendly and fun to watch, they're not often seen in zoos.

If you visit the polar bears in the summer, you'll see that they have a cold shower running all the time. They may even have chunks of ice to sit on! That's because they come from the far, far North and don't like hot weather.

But monkeys like hot weather. You'll never see them outdoors in cold weather. They're kept in warm houses because they're used to living in hot jungles.

Animals need good food, water, clean houses, and love. Just like people!